STEWART

ISLAND

Dry riverbed, upper Rakeahua River

Leave only footprints

STEWART ISLAND

The Last Refuge

PHOTOGRAPHY

Erwin Brinkmann

TEXT

Neville Peat

RANDOM HOUSE
NEW ZEALAND LTD

Random House New Zealand Ltd
(An imprint of the Random House Group)

18 Poland Road
Glenfield
Auckland 10
New Zealand

Associated companies, branches and representatives
throughout the world.

First published 1992
© Erwin Brinkmann and Neville Peat 1992
ISBN 1 86941 165 X

Typeset by Typocrafters Ltd, Auckland
Printed in Hong Kong

All rights reserved. No part of this publication may be
reproduced or transmitted in any form or by any means,
electronic or mechanical, including photocopying, recording,
storage in any information retrieval system or otherwise,
without the written permission of the publisher.

For Arianne
(EB)

For Mary and Sophora
(NP)

The authors acknowledge with gratitude the support of
Bruce and Sue Ford, proprietors of the South Sea Hotel;
in particular, the flights Bruce provided over the island
by light aircraft.

The *Manurere* leaving port

CONTENTS

Acknowledgements/8

Preface/9

One/13
Island of Superlatives

Two/30
The Settled Parts

Three/48
Coast to Coast

Four/68
Forest Tall

Five/80
The High Ground

Six/93
Islands of Last Resort

Seven/103
'Piece of the Primeval'

Select Bibliography/114

Index/116

Bivouac at Doughboy Bay

ACKNOWLEDGEMENTS

The authors thank the following for their various contributions: Margaret Hopkins (archival research); Lindsay Hazley (historic photographs); Pat and Merv King, John Leask, Alan Gray, Gary Neave, Simon Marwick (transport by sea); Ann Marwick (typing of captions). The encouragement and advice of Julia Brooke-White and Ron and Elspeth Tindal is also acknowledged. Rod Morris provided the kakapo illustration.

Information on aspects of Stewart Island natural history was willingly given by the following Department of Conservation personnel: Greg Lind, Robin Thomas, Jane Hare, Rogan Colbourne, Andy Roberts, Andy Cox, Brian Rance and Brian Patrick and Graeme Loh. John Dowding and Geoff Aimers also assisted with information. Advice on Maori history came from Russell Beck and Atholl Anderson.

The authors also acknowledge the work of generations of naturalists and scientists, starting with Dr David Lyall, surgeon aboard HMS *Acheron*, who made the first study of the plants of the island. In the 1870s, Charles Traill, with assistance from his brothers, Walter and Arthur, added valuable information, as did Thomas Kirk, Donald Petrie, G. M. Thomson, P. Goyen and W. S. Hamilton in the 1880s. Leonard Cockayne produced a landmark account of the island's plant life in 1909 following a series of visits in the preceding few years. It remained the most comprehensive account until the publication of Hugh Wilson's field guide in 1982 — a monumental work.

The geology and geomorphology of the island was reported on by such figures as Sir James Hector and Professor J. G. Black last century and by Dr Gordon Williams in this century.

Early observers of bird life included Herbert Guthrie-Smith and Lance Richdale.

The most recent studies of Stewart Island natural history have been undertaken by entomologists Brian Patrick and Barbara Barratt, and botanist Brian Rance. They made five trips to the alpine regions of the island between 1986 and 1988, and published their report in 1992. In it, they acknowledged the pioneering work of entomologist Alfred Philpott.

Herries Beattie documented Maori lore and place names, and historian Basil Howard produced a full account of post-European settlement for the Stewart Island Centennial Committee.

PREFACE

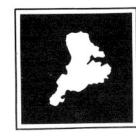

Erwin Brinkmann's Stewart Island is a glorious jostle of patterns, colours, textures and light plays, from the panoramic to the particular. His images reflect the diverse landforms, waterways, vegetation types and coastal scenery to be found there — diverse to the point of astonishing. He pursues these images with the diligence and careful attention of a hunter-gatherer.

One warm November afternoon, on the track from Port Pegasus to the top of the Tin Range, Erwin and I paused at a stream in the forest. The stream at this point tumbled over a bank and disappeared into a dark pool overhung by trees. Running water does mysterious things in a sylvan setting, and so I spent a few moments observing the whole scene — the volume and depth of water, the lie of the land, and the nature of the surrounding forest.

Then I realised Erwin was engrossed in something else, something close-up. He was at a crouch on the little bridge, examining the pattern of froth on the sluggish upstream side and the way a fern frond dipped its tip into the eyebrow-like skiffs of froth. In short order he had framed up an image that summarised, exquisitely, the essence of the stream.

In the process of taking this picture he seemed to melt into the surrounds. This was due not so much to his being 'at one' with the forest, or the need to keep still, but rather to the colour of his attire — virtually all of it green. On his excursions into the wilds of Stewart Island, Erwin likes to wear green things: green shirt, jacket and raincoat, green pack: even green gumboots. He looks comfortable — in his element.

Things did not start out this way, however. When Erwin first came to the island for a fortnight's tramping, he set out to walk the northern circuit — and hated it. A self-confessed city boy from an urban country (Holland, not much bigger in area than Canterbury, had fifteen million people), and managing a restaurant-tearooms business in Lyttelton at the time, he found the tracks too steep in places, too muddy and too prone to flooding. 'Why', he asked himself, 'are the tracks not properly maintained?'

But at Mason Bay, in the second week, he was hut-bound by heavy rain, and, forced to contemplate the experience, he began to find merit in it after all. Back at Lyttelton he thought about seeing if there was work available in the Stewart Island wilderness. The Lands and Survey Department took him on as a parks and reserves assistant, and straight away he began taking photographs in the hope a book might eventuate.

About a year into the project he baulked at the idea. The more he saw of the island, the more difficult the task looked. How could he hope to do an honest job of portraying the island's diverse nature when the majority of its natural assets were closeted by rough untracked terrain and rough weather?

Slowly, though, his portfolio of photographs increased and gaps began to be filled. He realised that every time he got off the beaten track he was likely to find something new, and that certain shots, requiring the right weather, right season and right light conditions, might take weeks, months or even years to secure. In the process he might have to put up with not a little adversity.

STEWART ISLAND

Years went by before he was satisfied with his one good shot on Mount Anglem. At Mason Bay one time, with his partner Arianne, he waited two weeks for a picture . . . 'At eight o'clock one evening, the sun suddenly broke through; we rushed to the river (Duck Creek) and got it.'

Winter photography is especially dicey. Erwin was determined to capture hoar frost on the Freshwater Flats, but good light and hoar frost do not get on — the morning sun will quickly eliminate the vestiges of frost. The timing is down to minutes, if not seconds. He had to camp on the Flats and move smartly to the wetlands area as dawn was breaking.

The Table Hill–Tin Range alpine zone, home of cloud and gales, presented the severest challenge. Anyone venturing on to Table Hill and the Tin Range is advised to walk the tops in one day, or risk getting caught in a storm. Needing to catch first light and last light for the sake of potent photography, Erwin had no choice. He took a tent, and Arianne joined him.

They made four trips to that high ground in the south, planning to stay out only one night each time. On three of the four trips — the first three — they struck foul weather.

A thick, damp fog plagued the first trip and they had to navigate by compass to extricate themselves. The second visit

Photographing a shellbank in Cooks Arm, Port Pegasus   **Neville** Peat

Blechnum sp.

PREFACE

Rakeahua River

started auspiciously; the day was bathed in sunshine and they celebrated by swimming in the tarn below the Mount Allen summit. But in the middle of the night, a big wind burst upon their campsite and heavy rain forced them to move their tent. The storm continued for two more days — three nights altogether. They could go nowhere. Having to support the tent poles in the gale, they hardly slept. The third day was better and they hurried out.

On the third trip they camped at Blaikies Hill. About five in the morning their tent collapsed in a furious nor'wester. As Erwin reported: 'We tried to walk but just kept on getting blown off our feet. All we could do was get down in the tussock and wrap ourselves in the tent. But that didn't stop us getting colder and colder. I thought we'd be stuck there for days. Then the wind stopped. Just like that. Sudden. Sheer luck.'

They scrambled out to Rakeahua Hut in the valley to the north, only to meet another challenge — a swollen and still-rising Rakeahua River. Erwin estimated the river at about three metres above its usual height. Water had almost reached the hut.

The Rakeahua, in common with other rivers on Stewart Island, floods with little notice. And the fact that it falls as quickly is no comfort if you happen to have tied up your dinghy in anticipation of normal levels — as Erwin and Arianne had done before setting out for Blaikies Hill . . . 'In the circumstances there was no option but to cut the line. Most of it was hidden in the floodwaters. At least we had taken the precaution of putting the outboard motor in the hut. So you cut the line, and next thing you are swimming madly to try to get control of the dinghy. You're in the tree-tops, and the river — well, it is flowing like hell.'

Before going to Stewart Island, Erwin had never explored wild places without the aid of established tracks and bridges. Now, with compass and map, he will tackle almost any part of the island, and has learnt to be guided, as to altitude and position relative to the coast or inland waterways, by the nature of the vegetation. For coastal photography, he works the tides, knowing that some places offer brilliant images at low tide and others look better with the tide in.

Cooks Arm at Port Pegasus, a narrow, meandering inlet that transforms to mudflats over much of its length at low tide, is a favourite spot of his: 'There's no place like it anywhere in New Zealand; it's absolutely superb.'

The wilderness nature of the island is keenly felt by Erwin. 'There are places you can go where you know you're the first one to visit in a year. You can feel the remoteness and the tension, too, as if at any moment you might suddenly see a bird from the past. Stewart Island is the kind of place that *feels* like a last refuge. I wonder if this was where moa and laughing owls ended their days. As for kokako, I'm always looking out for signs and listening out for its call.'

He worries about the trend towards taming wild places when what is needed, for sanity's sake, is a policy to keep large areas natural and undeveloped — without tracks, signs, huts or other human intrusions. He likes the idea of having places to explore, places that cannot be reached without physical effort and perhaps some discomfort.

In collecting the images for this book, Erwin Brinkmann would happily admit he found pleasure in the discomfort.

Neville Peat

ONE

Island of Superlatives

Stewart Island, whose Maori name is Rakiura, is routinely described as the southernmost and smallest of the three main islands of New Zealand. This is true enough. But Stewart Island has more superlatives to offer than the simple geographic ones. It is the least modified of the three main islands — the least logged, burnt and built on. In other words, the most natural. For scenic quality, the island also excels, although most visitors see just a fraction of it — the forest-fringed bays and beaches of the north-east sector, the coastline facing the South Island. Pioneer botanist Leonard Cockayne, who roamed Stewart Island early this century, collecting and recording, was inspired to write in 1909:

> It is hard to speak of the scenery of Stewart Island without using a superabundance of superlatives.

Cockayne's opinion still holds. If anything, he might be even more impressed now. In his day, sawmilling had a foothold on the northern side of Paterson Inlet (the last mill closed in 1931). Farming was going on at Mason Bay then, too, but since 1987 it has been confined to the Horseshoe Bay area and, to a lesser extent, The Neck.

Thus, for scenery and vegetation, Stewart Island is much the way it was when humans first set foot upon its fascinating shores, probably a thousand years ago.

*

Roughly triangular, the island is about 75 kilometres long by 45 kilometres wide. Flat land is limited. Hills, rising to ranges in places, extend from coast to coast. Mount Anglem (980 metres), near the northern end, is the highest point — an outstanding feature on a clear day. The coastline, totalling 755 kilometres, is deeply indented. Paterson Inlet (100 square kilometres) encroaches halfway across the island, and other safe harbours in the east include Port Adventure and Port Pegasus.

The coastline is spectacular, ranging in nature from estuarine mudflats gently nudged by the tide to granite bluffs that receive without respite the pounding, lashing swells of deep ocean. Wave-cut rock platforms or banks of boulders may give way suddenly to sand. Commonly the sand is fine-grained and creamy in colour; but some beaches sport other hues — golden, orange-red, black with iron, or blinding white.

On the steeper sheltered shores is to be found perhaps the most enduring image of Stewart Island — trees and shrubs overhanging the sea, undisturbed, haven-like, safe from clearance for farming or plantation forestry. Tree daisies festoon the scene in summer with billowing white flowers. And when they decide to flower, robust southern rata trees drape scarlet blooms over the tide.

Everywhere the forest presses forward with vigour to greet the sea — that uncompromising boundary for land plants. And

STEWART ISLAND

Sunrise over Dynamite Point, Paterson Inlet

in reply, at every charge of the tide, the sea demonstrates its own irresistible power. It speaks with many voices, hissing over sand, gurgling through boulders, booming against cliffs — dictating terms. For Stewart Island is an oceanic island, lying between latitudes 46 and 47 degrees south in the zone of the great west-wind drift. There is nothing but wind-driven sea in either direction, east or west, right around the globe, except where it meets the southern tip of South America and a few specks of land that call themselves sub-Antarctic islands.

To the south of Stewart Island, and well out of sight of each other, are New Zealand's own sub-Antarctic outposts. The closest are the Snares Islands, about 100 kilometres away, and beyond this group are the Auckland Islands and Campbell Island. Next stop, Antarctica.

Who said this was Planet Earth? The planet is two-thirds ocean, and nowhere is this more obvious than in the latitudes embracing Stewart Island, the fabled Roaring Forties. Westerly winds prevail right around the globe in these latitudes, and the ocean currents tend in the same direction. Thus the west coast of Stewart Island is the weather coast, but the whole island experiences an oceanic climate that is cool, moist and not subject to the extremes felt by larger land masses.

The mean annual temperature is just on ten degrees Celsius. Frosts and snowfalls are infrequent, although snow may lie on the peaks for a few weeks. In September 1916, to the astonishment of everyone, a heavy snowfall crushed forest at sea level. Such events are rare, however. The island — its north-eastern shores at least — generally enjoy a milder climate than coastal regions north of Foveaux Strait.

An ocean current originating in the Tasman Sea, far to the north, is credited with moderating the island's weather. As the current heads south past Fiordland, seeking a passage west, it splits in two to bathe both sides of Stewart Island, with the northern arm of the current driving water through Foveaux Strait. Thus, in the vicinity of Stewart Island there is a mixing of sub-Antarctic waters and warmer waters from the north.

Nonetheless, the climate is not uniform throughout. The

Rockface, Doughboy Bay beach

island is large enough (1,740 square kilometres, including offshore islands) for there to be significant local variation. The north-east side of the triangle, including Paterson Inlet and the inhabited areas, is distinctly drier and sunnier than southern areas.

In the south and west, annual rainfall is estimated to reach the 5,000-millimetre mark — five metres — whereas the average figure for Halfmoon Bay is only 1,600 millimetres. May and June are the wettest months, but rain is well spread through the year. Halfmoon Bay averages 210 rain days.

In common with other oceanic islands, Stewart Island is frequently cloudy — at least, the ranges tend to collect cloud. South of Paterson Inlet, the cloud cover is more persistent.

But wind holds the whiphand climatically. Plants and animals have had to evolve mechanisms to cope with the formidable westerlies — the chill and dehydration factors, the buffeting, the airborne salt. Wind conspires with the erosive forces of rain and chemical weathering to attack rock, and on western shores it shifts great hills of sand hundreds of metres inland.

The first people here named not only the peaks, rivers, bays, fishing spots, trees and birds, but also the winds. Historian Herries Beattie recorded Maori names for no fewer than fourteen winds. The west-north-west wind was known as wawa-waiau and also as hau-mate, the death wind, for it upset canoes. Pu-ta-taki was the name for the wind from the south-south-east, renowned for bearing rain.

Gale-force winds are more common on the ranges than at the coast, as Leonard Cockayne reported from his botanising expeditions in the early 1900s:

> When it blew so furiously on Mount Anglem as to make it almost impossible to stand upright on the exposed alpine meadow, at Halfmoon Bay there was a calm day.

Yet in an average year, Halfmoon Bay will experience gale-force winds on fourteen days. A westerly gale belting down Paterson Inlet is something to behold.

*

When the weather is fine, Stewart Island becomes an emerald isle in an immense blue cradle of sea and sky. The temptation is strong to get out and explore the distant peaks and beyond. But any map of the island is likely to daunt the exploring ambitions of all but the hardiest trampers. There are no roads except for a few small squiggles around Halfmoon and Horseshoe Bays. This is not Waiheke Island or Chatham Island. No permanent settlement exists beyond Halfmoon and Horseshoe Bays. The island is a wilderness. And even the northern tramping circuit, taking eight to ten days to complete, encompasses only about a third of the island.

The only way to glimpse the diverse nature of the island is to get in the air. A two-hour flight, clockwise around the island, produces such impressions as . . . *Paterson Inlet*, virtually an inland sea with numerous forest-girt embayments, broad arms and sufficient water and safe anchorages for the biggest navies and fishing fleets . . . *Port Adventure*, name matching nature, whose most secluded parts bear names such as Abrahams Bosom and Oyster Cove, and alluring crescents of coloured sand . . . *Lords River*, navigable for several kilometres, remote as a waterway deep in the Brazilian jungle . . . *Toitoi Flat*, a dullish-brown circle of wetlands surrounded by forested hills and drained by a river whose rapids — turning billy-tea water white — hint of a steeper and more broken terrain than is apparent from the air . . . *Mount Allen* (750 metres), the island's second-highest peak, brown-browed, overlooking an area dotted with weird humps of grey rock that protrude, naked, from patchy bush, last refuge of the kakapo . . . *Port Pegasus*, guarded by three islands that afford four entrances for shipping, and flanked by more bare knobs and cones of granite . . . *South Cape*, white-wreathed by surf, leaping-off place for the sub-Antarctic . . . *Big South Cape Island*, largest of the muttonbird islands, its lower slopes cloaked in muttonbird scrub . . . on up the west coast now; *Easy Harbour*, a sliver of unruffled water but how safe in a storm? (the sealing brig *Industry* was lost here in 1831, the first recorded shipwreck in Stewart Island waters) . . . *Doughboy Bay*, biscuit-coloured sand piled high against forested hills . . . *Mason Bay*, a great curve of sand backed by enormous sandhills that testify to its antiquity . . . *Ruggedy Mountains*, rock pinnacles in close formation sprouting from the sea, sienna tinged and interspersed with bush . . . inland now, bypassing the brilliant forest-bound beaches of northern coast and heading for home; the *Ruggedy Flats*, a surprising expanse of flat country, but thoroughly wet, with little lakes in abundance . . . *Paterson Inlet* again, and the airstrip on the levelled hill overlooking the inlet, cut out of the bush, fitting the wilderness image.

Paterson Inlet and the flats to the west — the Ruggedy Flats and those associated with the Freshwater River — occupy a fault-affected depression in the land (geologically speaking, a graben) that all but divides the island. Between the Freshwater Flats and Mason Bay on the west coast there is a low saddle, a gateway for the sea if sea levels rise in the future.

About a third of the island, centred on the Anglem Massif, lies to the north of Paterson Inlet and the flats. To the south

ISLAND OF SUPERLATIVES

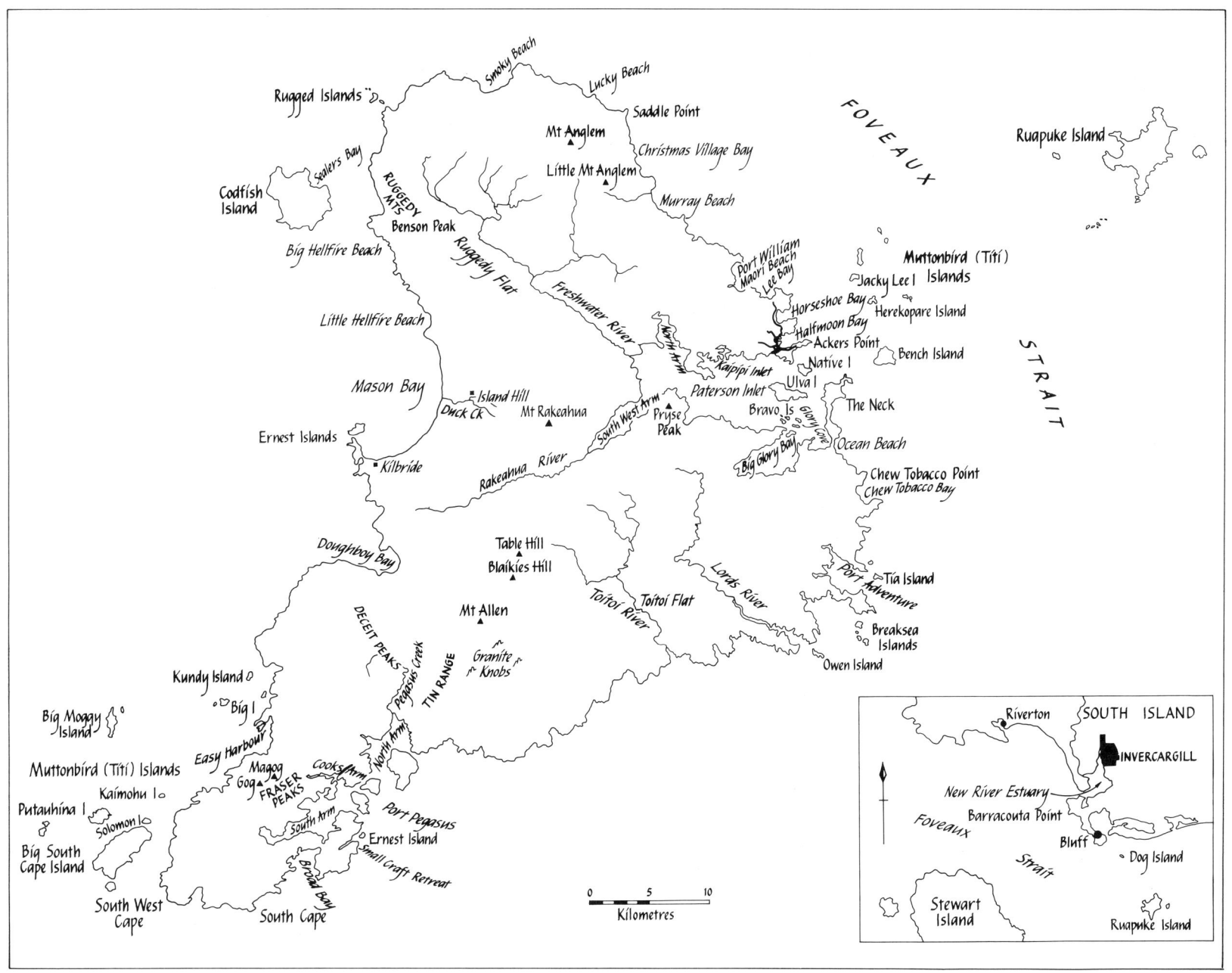

STEWART ISLAND

Eroded granite slabs, Pegasus area

are the hilly solitudes of the Tin Range, Table Hill and Mount Rakeahua. The bulk of the island is built of granite that intruded, semi-molten, into the original crust from the core of the earth about 100 million years ago. Stewart Island is the tip of a granite 'iceberg'. Fiordland and the Snares Islands share a similar geological origin.

The Anglem third of the island is comprised of allied igneous rocks called biotite and tonalite, which are related to rocks forming the land around Bluff, Riverton and the Longwoods in Southland. The southern (Rakeahua) granites, coarse-grained, speckled and liable to shine with feldspar crystals, are similar in nature to the Fiordland rocks. Filling the gap between the two hilly regions is a complex concoction called the Paterson group, which includes sedimentary schist, much older than the granite, perhaps over 300 million years old. Schist gravels come in handy as a dressing on paths and as an aggregate in concrete, hence the extraction of them from the Bravo Islands in Paterson Inlet over the years. The Paterson rocks extend west at least as far as Codfish Island, which combines elements of both the Rakeahua granite and the Paterson complex.

In the south, the granite does not completely dominate the landscape. Remnants of the original crust, again substantially schist, help form the Tin Range. Last century the tin-tungsten lodes in the schist and scattered deposits of wolframite and cassiterite, together with some gold and monazite, tempted miners.

Over millions of years tectonic forces have not only uplifted the island (the mountains probably reached their present height about ten million years ago) but tilted it into the bargain — dipping its eastern edges into the sea.

As a result, most of the rain that falls on the island flows eastward in the streams and rivers. The biggest rivers, the Rakeahua and Freshwater, which empty into Paterson Inlet, rise almost on the western shores of the island.

Combine the tilting effect with a phenomenal rise in sea levels in ancient times and the result is a drowned landscape

ISLAND OF SUPERLATIVES

Patterns on dune

and the truncation of Stewart Island from the South Island. Paterson Inlet was once a river valley and the Rakeahua and Freshwater Rivers were mere tributaries of a much bigger river that had its mouth beyond The Neck. On the sea floor east of the inlet's heads is evidence of the path the river once took beyond the present shoreline.

Foveaux Strait has come and gone in ages past, owing to fluctuations in ocean volumes. At present its minimum width is twenty-seven kilometres (a line drawn between Saddle Point on the island's northern coast and Barracouta Point north-west of Bluff).

In the last ice age (14,000 to 20,000 years ago), with much of the world's fresh water locked up on land, sea levels were about 180 metres lower than they are today. Coastlines bore little resemblance to present ones. Britain was joined to France, the Bering Strait was dry and all three main islands of New Zealand were joined by land bridges. About 14,000 years ago, a few thousand years earlier than other parts of the world, New Zealand's glacial ice began to melt and retreat. Sea levels rose as a consequence, and the land between South and Stewart Islands, an old alluvial plain created by the great rivers of Southland, was submerged. Foveaux Strait, in its present form, is less than 10,000 years old. Its floor is covered in coarse pebbles, sand and shell fragments.

The strait is relatively shallow, with depths in the order of twenty to forty metres on the ferry route between Bluff and Halfmoon Bay. The oyster beds in the strait are found in water shallow enough to be inspected by professional divers. Soundings show the strait is shallowest on a line drawn through the northern Muttonbird (Titi) Islands and Ruapuke Island. Presumably this is where the ancient bridge gave way to the rising ocean.

*

Maori lore explains the creation of Foveaux Strait in rather different terms. Far back in time there lived a whale named Kiwa (also known as Kewa or Kiwha) whose bulk and appetite were prodigious. It was Kiwa who created the strait simply by chewing through the land bridge. For evidence of this look to Solander Island. That chunky piece of rock west of the strait, 300 metres high, is a tooth of Kiwa's, loosened in the process and spat out. Accordingly, Foveaux Strait is Te Ara a Kiwa, the Pathway of Kiwa. (In Maori tradition Kiwa is also the name of an early navigator.)

Several traditional names apply to Stewart Island. Te Punga o Te Waka a Maui — the Anchor of Maui's Canoe — refers to the exploits of the demigod Maui, who fished up the North Island from a great canoe now known as the South Island. Stewart Island, at its southern end, is the anchor. Another name for the island, deriving from more recent tradition, is Mouterenui — Big Island. Its size in this case is relative to Codfish Island, which was known as Whenuahou — Newfoundland. Several hundred years ago this was a landfall and the site of a settlement.

But the name that is commonly applied to the island is Rakiura. Freely translated, Rakiura means 'land of glowing skies', and most people have assumed the name is inspired by the sunsets. Alternatively, it might refer to the displays of aurora, fairly common in the night sky over the island, the island being closer to the south polar region — home of Aurora Australis, the Southern Lights — than is the rest of New Zealand.

Rakiura is actually an abbreviation of a name that recalls a love story. According to Herries Beattie, an ardent recorder of Maori place-names and their origin, the story involves a suitor named Te Rakitamau who came to the island to ask a local chief for the hand of the older of his two daughters. On finding she was betrothed, he blushed — and he blushed deeper than ever when he was refused the hand of the second daughter, who as it happens was also promised in marriage to another. Thus arose the name, Te Rakiura a Te Rakitamau — The Blushing Day (or Sky) of Te Rakitamau. Aurora or sunset, the blushing persists in the sky over the island at day's end.

In summer the island enjoys longer days than anywhere else

in New Zealand thanks to its southerly location. Around summer solstice, there is still light at ten thirty, and the dawn will start the new day less than six hours later.

Perhaps, in applying the name Aotearoa (commonly translated as 'Land of the Long White Cloud') to the islands of New Zealand, the Polynesian discoverers were referring not to the extent of the cloud but to the extent of the daylight. How surprising the daylight must have been for a people from the tropics, used to near-equal hours of daylight and dark.

The early people camped on beaches, river mouths and strategic headlands all around Rakiura, but signs of permanent large settlements are few. There appears to have been a lot of travel across the strait. Archaeologists have recovered many tools and weapons made of stone not found on the island, including pounamu (greenstone) and argillite. Pounamu was worked on the island. Among the tools in use were adzes, chisels, drill points and knives. There were moa-skinning knives and smaller knives made of a transparent quartz called rock crystal. The use of rock crystal for these small blades — prehistoric pocket-knives — is distinctive. The people further north would more commonly fashion their blades from obsidian. New technology developed by northern tribes over generations tended not to filter down to the Rakiura Maori, who retained their older-style tools almost up to the period of European contact.

Clearly, the food resources of Rakiura and its adjacent islands made the voyage across the strait by canoe — the ocean-going double canoes or smaller craft — worthwhile. Fish and shellfish abounded, and the Maori ate what is prized today — blue cod, crayfish, paua and oysters. The oysters were easily harvested from the rocks at Port Adventure and roasted, like mussels, over a fire. Seals, too, were taken. Forest produce included the roots and shoots of certain ferns, and in summer the delicious berries of kotukutuku, the tree fuchsia, and tataramoa, the blackberry-like native bush lawyer.

There was good eating to be had from several birds of the forest — notably kereru (pigeon) and kaka, the parrot. Large, flightless moa, before they disappeared, provided sustenance in bulk. Bones of Euryapteryx, medium-sized moa standing about one and a half metres high, are common in Rakiura middens, and moa-shell fragments have also been dug up. There is a nagging doubt, though, about whether the moa eaten by the Rakiura Maori were transported as carcasses to the island (and the shell brought in as water containers) or whether they were hunted there. No moa bones have been found to date in a natural (rather than cultural) setting. Until such a find is made, the doubt will remain. But it is reasonable to assume moa lived on the island. The long history of a land bridge would suggest this, and the island offered suitable habitat — lowland forest, scrub and grasslands.

Above all, though, the Maori were attracted to Rakiura for its resource of titi — now more usually called muttonbird. Chicks of the ubiquitous sooty shearwater were harvested *en masse* in autumn, then cooked and preserved in their own fat. The titi harvest became an industry of immense importance, not only for the food value — preserved titi would keep for twelve months — but also for the sake of trade: titi for greenstone, or eels from Canterbury, or other items coveted in the south. The Rakiura Maori had it down to a fine art, this titi business, and their descendants have maintained the tradition of annual visits to the Muttonbird Islands. Tens of thousands of sooty shearwater chicks are taken every year.

In the past, the Maori of the deep south must have relied to a large extent on titi to see them through the winter, for their lands were too cold to support crops of kumara. In fact, Rakiura is about as far south as Polynesian culture extended in pre-European times. Although adzes have been found on the Snares Islands to the south, and southern traditions speak of fishing expeditions to the Snares, it is hard to imagine a substantial Maori presence ever developing on these small sub-Antarctic islands out of sight of the mainland.

In the early days of European contact, the focus of Maori life was not Rakiura but the largest of the Foveaux Strait islands — Ruapuke.

STEWART ISLAND

Sand pattern in creek bed

ISLAND OF SUPERLATIVES

Flax surrounded by jointed rush

STEWART ISLAND

*

Europeans knew nothing of the southern region of New Zealand until Lieutenant (later Captain) James Cook, Royal Navy, mapped them in 1770 in the course of circumnavigating New Zealand in the barque *Endeavour*.

The first week of March found the *Endeavour* well down the east coast of the South Island, but too far out to sea to identify a separate island. Only a few landmarks were named — Bench Island (Ruapuke), South Cape and a few rocks east of South Cape appropriately named The Traps after they almost ended the *Endeavour*'s voyage.

By 11 March the *Endeavour* was in Te Waewae Bay (Southland) and bound for the western seaboard. The question of whether another major island had been rounded was much on the minds of the senior personnel on board. Cook took a cautious view — no doubt wary of sending ships into uncharted waters — and drew a pair of dotted lines on the map instead of indicating a strait. Although earlier of the opinion that a strait existed, he did an about-turn, declaring:

> . . . from the several bearings I had taken it appeared there was but little reason to suppose it an Id., on the Contrary I hardly have a doubt but what it joins to and makes part of the main land.

For the rest of that century the wider maritime world would be oblivious to the existence of a strait.

The rounding of South Cape, however, resolved a geographic issue of great interest to European scientists and explorers — whether the Southern Hemisphere contained a landmass to counterbalance the Northern Hemisphere continents. Abel Tasman, European discoverer of New Zealand in the previous century, had hinted at the possibility that he had charted, in part, *Terra Australis Incognita* — the Unknown South Land. Cook's expedition hoped to prove it. Certainly Joseph Banks, an explorer and naturalist on the *Endeavour*, held great hopes as they sailed down the east coast. But as the ship rounded South Cape on 10 March 1770 and headed into the Tasman Sea, Banks wrote:

> Blew fresh all day, but carried us round the Point to the total demolition of our aerial fabric called Continent.

New Zealand was not the promised land, not in a continental sense. But as Cook would report, following a second expedition in 1773, it was a land rich in resources. The southern regions offered seals and timber aplenty.

Within twenty years, sealing gangs were heading across the Tasman Sea from Port Jackson (Sydney) to harvest the New Zealand fur seal. They worked the Fiordland and South Westland coasts first. It was a secretive trade, this sealing, and no one can be sure which sealing expedition discovered Foveaux Strait. The evidence suggests it was an American sealer, O. F. Smith, who in 1804 reported to the Governor of New South Wales the existence of a strait. At the same time he supplied sketch maps of the main harbours of the east coast of the island lying to the south of it. None of this was published, though.

Five years later, in March 1809, Captain John Grono, of the sealing ship *Governor Bligh*, announced in the *Sydney Gazette* the existence of a 'new-discovered strait, called Foveaux Strait', named after the Governor of New South Wales. For a while it was known as 'Smith's Strait'. Grono described it as 'a very dangerous navigation from the numerous shoals, rocks and little islands with which it is crowded'. Grono did not name the island.

In August the same year, the Sydney-based sealing vessel *Pegasus*, under Captain Samuel Chase, sailed into the harbour that would eventually bear her name — Port Pegasus. Her first officer, William Stewart, made a detailed chart of the harbour and subsequently produced a chart of the whole island, which was published in the 1816 edition of the *Oriental Navigator* — the first known printed reference to Stewart Island.

William Stewart had at least one namesake in the Sydney

sealing trade who undertook sealing trips to sub-Antarctic Antipodes Island in 1805 and 1806, and for many years Stewart the chartmaker and Stewart the sealer were considered one and the same. Recent research has shown there were two Stewarts, the one for whom the island is named being the lesser known.

Sealing intensified as charts were published and the word got around. But by the end of the 1820s the trade was over. The seals were gone, plundered to the point of extinction. A new exploitive era took over — whaling.

The waters around Stewart Island drew whaling ships, and the seasonal nature of the work meant the whalers had time to tend gardens, cut timber, build whaleboats and establish families with Maori wives. Wrote historian Basil Howard:

Rakiura cast its spell upon the whalemen who ventured close to its shores, and thither they returned, one by one, to settle.

British sovereignty was claimed over 'Stewart's Island' on 21 May 1840 on the grounds of prior discovery — Cook's. The Treaty of Waitangi had been signed in February by representatives of the Crown and northern tribes, and a British vessel, HMS *Herald*, sailed south to collect signatures from southern chiefs.

Strangely, the *Herald* bypassed the small northern settlements of Stewart Island and made landfall at deserted Port Pegasus, where Her Majesty Queen Victoria's colours were hoisted and the declaration of sovereignty was buried on a small tidal island. Its location remains a mystery.

Colonisation made no difference initially to life on Stewart Island, which was deemed to lie beyond the bounds of civilisation, an outpost somewhere south of settled New Zealand. Not until 1864 did the Government stake a claim by purchasing the entire island — except for specified reserves — from the Rakiura Maori. The purchase was motivated more by the Government's desire to pre-empt private land deals than by any expressed interest in developing the place.

On the contrary, the Government would have found little encouraging news of the island's potential in the report of a coastal survey undertaken in 1850 and 1851 by HMS *Acheron*, a wooden paddle-sloop under orders from the British Admiralty to chart New Zealand coastal waters. The *Acheron* journal contained comments on Stewart Island such as:

An utter solitude . . . nought but rock-rock-rock-rock . . . rain-rain-rain — always rain . . . very monotonous scenery . . . There does not seem soil enough to nourish a potatoe.

Nonetheless, the birds and plants of Stewart Island did impress the explorers aboard the *Acheron*. The journal makes mention of several bird species, including the weka ('They abound in the neighbourhood of native villages and pahs, where they feed with domestic poultry'). *Acheron*'s Scottish surgeon, Dr David Lyall, an able naturalist, made the first collection of Stewart Island plants, some of which are named for him. They include the giant white buttercup (*Ranunculus lyallii*), a member of the carrot family (*Anisotome lyallii*) and a big-leafed herb that the Maori called punui (*Stilbocarpa lyallii*). Lyall found plants that occurred nowhere else. He put Stewart Island on another kind of map — the world of natural science.

*

The plants and animals of Stewart Island live in an environment as close to natural as can be found on mainland New Zealand. There is an aura of 'Old New Zealand' about it. Human inroads into the physical environment have been limited by poor soils, inaccessibility and remoteness from the main centres of population. Yet it is wrong to label the island pristine. Various introduced animals have wreaked havoc among native birds, notably ground birds or weak flyers, and disturbed the vegetation. Possums and deer (red and white-tailed) damage the forest; feral cats, Norway rats and ship rats

STEWART ISLAND

Boulder in stream

Stewart Island shag

attack birds and lizards. Even the smaller kiore, or Polynesian rat, introduced by the Maori centuries ago, has taken its toll. Thankfully, mice and the mustelid predators (ferret, stoat and weasel) have not as yet established on the island.

Despite the impacts, the island's plant life retains a character of its own. The diversity is extraordinary. Botanist Hugh Wilson has identified 160 different plant communities, inhabiting coastal marshes, dunes and bluffs, tall forest, short forest, scrubland, grassland, mountain bogs, rocky zones and alpine herbfields.

Wind has a lot to do with the vegetation patterns, but other governing factors include drainage, fog, soil fertility, altitude and proximity to the sea. What impressed botanists early on was the presence at sea level of plants with an alpine or sub-alpine habit farther north. The predominance of tree daisies, from the coastal fringes to the mountain scrublands, is also distinctive as is the absence of certain trees common north of Foveaux Strait. Beech trees are nowhere to be seen in the forest — a remarkable thing given their predominance in western Southland. Native cedar, kanuka, celery pine and lemonwood are also missing.

That the plants of Stewart Island live in a world of their own is evident from the number of endemics. Twenty-eight species are unique to the island. Six of them are coastal; most are herbs or dwarf shrubs inhabiting the upland areas, including three Celmisia daisies and three species of spaniard, or speargrass.

Some endemic species are found only to the south of Paterson Inlet, and some are found only on the high ground to the north — a separation that may be due to the island's split geological personality.

If the island's flora is full of surprises, its fauna is equally strange and special. The birdlife reeks of rarity, from the critically endangered kakapo on Codfish Island to the New Zealand dotterels that breed on the mountain tops. South Island saddlebacks are defying extinction on a handful of predator-free offshore islands, but what of the South Island kokako? Does it still exist? The Stewart Island forests may be hiding the last one or two.

Brown kiwis — the Stewart Island sub-species — seem to be holding their own, assertive to the point of leaving their burrows in daylight hours to feed. But there is concern about the survival of another flightless bird, the Stewart Island weka. Far back in time, the New Zealand mainlands once moved with land birds that evolved a flightless or weak-flying status in the absence of predatory mammals, but the arrival of rats, cats and mustelids put many to the wall of extinction. It says something about the natural values of Stewart Island that the last wild population of kakapo, the big forest parrot, should be found here.

As for seabirds, Stewart Island claims no fewer than twenty-one species. If New Zealand is the seabird capital of the world, Stewart Island is central square. Take the penguins: three species (yellow-eyed, little blue and Fiordland crested) breed on the island and its outliers, and several more are liable to visit, including Snares crested, erect-crested, rockhopper and king. Albatrosses, notably the Shy and Buller's mollymawks and an occasional royal albatross, roam the seas around Stewart Island. Three petrel species and two prions are among the many seabirds breeding here, and the shag (cormorant) family is well represented by five breeding species — black, pied, little, blue and Stewart Island. Despite the annual muttonbird harvest, sooty shearwaters, or titi, return in their millions to nest on the offshore islands.

The seas around Stewart Island also support a variety of marine mammals — dolphins, whales and seals. Bottlenose dolphins, in schools of up to forty, are common inshore. They often enter Paterson Inlet, and sometimes they have calves with them. Occasionally, southern right whales enter too, to rest or calve. Sperm and pilot whales are known to cruise by the island, and pods of orcas (killer whales) are not uncommon in Foveaux Strait.

The seals have made a comeback since the trade in their fur plundered their colonies. Fur seals are found all around the island. There is a large colony of over 1,500 on Codfish Island. Hooker's sea lions, a rare breed, have established a colony at the head of Small Craft Retreat opposite Ernest Island, near Port Pegasus, and they regularly haul out at Ernest Island. Unlike fur seals, which inhabit rocky shores, the larger sea lions haul out on sand. They are not shy of human settlement. Ringaringa and Bathing Beach have been visited by sea lions in recent years. Leopard seals, common in Antarctic waters, are rarer visitors to the island.

In the sheltered waters of Pegasus, Port Adventure and Paterson Inlet live animals with ancestry going back 600 million years — filter-feeding shellfish called brachiopods, or lampshells. Their extensive beds are relatively intact for one good reason: to humans they taste foul.

Much of the fauna of Stewart Island is formally protected under national wildlife laws. Indeed, about ninety per cent of the land enjoys protection of one sort or another, mainly as nature reserves or scenic reserves administered by the Department of Conservation. Compared to the other two main islands of New Zealand, Rakiura is one big park. And in this park of superlative natural values, kiwis outnumber people.

TWO

The Settled Parts

When Stewart Islanders say they are 'going to town' they mean a trip to Invercargill. When they speak of 'the other side' they have the land across the strait, the South Island, in mind. These are the expressions of people who perceive their community to be not only small but also tangibly removed from mainstream New Zealand society.

The population — like that of many a native bird species — is just holding its own. For years it has hovered around the 400 mark. The inevitable loss of the younger generation to high schools and jobs in Invercargill or other South Island centres has been offset since the early 1980s by the advent of marine farming in Big Glory Bay, Paterson Inlet — the raising of salmon in moored sea cages and, on a smaller scale, mussels on lines attached to rafts. Fishing and tourism, with marine farming, keep New Zealand's southernmost village quietly ticking over.

Commercial fishing is the island's leading industry and the one with the longest history. The money is made from crayfish (rock lobster), a highly priced delicacy and top export earner, and blue cod, a succulent fish much in demand for the New Zealand market.

The cod are caught in pots, as are crayfish, or on handlines. Two fish factories on the island add value to the catch. In keeping with the scale of the place and for practical reasons, fishing boats are of modest size. They have to manoeuvre close

John Leask and son Danny lifting crayfish pots

to rocks to lay and lift pots. No long-range deep-sea trawlers hog the mooring space here.

Because fishing, in the main, is the work of men, the women left at home tend to be handy and diversified in their skills. Some women become wharfies. Some join the volunteer fire brigade. Island life teaches resourcefulness.

Halfmoon Bay is a safe anchorage for Stewart Island's fishing fleet

STEWART ISLAND

Most people live in the Halfmoon Bay (Oban) area — a picturesque amphitheatre. Business premises occupy front stage, lining up on an apron of flat land just beyond the sandy beach — hotel, general store, post office, cafe, souvenir shop and travel centre. The houses of Oban peep out of the bush on a dress circle of surrounding hills. To the north, Horseshoe Bay has its own collection of houses, plus a wharf and fish factory. To the south, around Golden Bay and Thule Bay on Paterson Inlet, there are more houses couched in bush.

Stewart Island has only about twenty-five kilometres of roading, which makes the Sunday drive a limited experience here. Many families own two cars — a rusty 'old bomb' for short runs on the island and a 'flash car' that is stored at Bluff or Invercargill for use on the other side.

There is a colourful touch to Stewart Island tarseal. Flecks of paua shell caught up in the aggregate are embedded in the seal, causing it to sparkle in the sunlight. The irony is that only pedestrians are able to appreciate the iridescence.

Of course, for thousands of visitors, walking is what Stewart Island is all about. What it lacks in roads, the island makes up for in walkways and tramping trails. Stretched out, they would extend for 160 kilometres. Around Halfmoon and Horseshoe Bays the shorter walks explore headlands, coastline and dense forest, and can keep visitors amused for days. Dedicated trampers have the northern circuit, with an option to climb Mount Anglem part-way round, to test them.

The island also attracts visitors keen on deer hunting, diving and fishing, and a few are now coming specially to see kiwis in the wild. Evening tours to Ocean Beach, south of The Neck, expect to find New Zealand's national bird feeding on hoppers and other invertebrates in the sand. At Mason Bay, kiwis are commonly seen searching the tussock flats for food in daylight hours. Some people need no excuse at all to visit the island other than an interest in savouring island life — and to say they have been there.

In December 1991, the island's tourist trade took on a new dimension with the arrival of a fast, fifty-passenger catamaran. The *Foveaux Express* plies the ferry route between Bluff and Halfmoon Bay — one hour each way, a speed undreamed of by earlier generations of islanders. The flight from Invercargill to Ryans Creek airstrip takes twenty minutes. Whether by sea or air, the journey involves an involuntary leap of the imagination. For a city-dweller, it is out of this world.

*

Halfmoon Bay is literally not what it seems. That name belongs to Horseshoe Bay and its magnificent curve of sand. And Horseshoe Bay more properly describes the outline of the island's main bay. The switch in names occurred a long time ago.

A chart from the 1844 survey voyage by the *Deborah*, under Captain Thomas Wing, shows Horseshoe Bay to be where Oban now is. But the names of the two bays were transposed on an 1857 chart produced by the British Admiralty — and transposed they have remained.

Ten years later, in 1867, the Southland Provincial Council unveiled a master plan for the island in which it had townships sprouting up everywhere — Halfmoon Bay, Kaipipi, Glory Cove, Chew Tobacco Bay, Port Adventure, Lords River, Port Pegasus, Easy Cove, Mason Bay and Port William. The optimism, fired by the pastoral farming ethic, was misplaced. Not only did the authorities fail to survey the land properly, but the settlers were beaten by the soil before they started. It was simply too wet and infertile, and its acidity could not be curbed by a regime of liming, as there were no known limestone deposits on the island. Only Halfmoon Bay eventuated as a village.

Farming never gained more than a toehold on the island, with small holdings of sheep and cattle around Halfmoon and Horseshoe Bays and The Neck, and two sheep runs on the flats behind Mason Bay (Island Hill and Kilbride). The 4,000-hectare Island Hill farm was closed by the Department of Conservation in 1987 after its sheep were shorn and killed, and the flats allowed to revert to their red-tussock cover. Farming on

THE SETTLED PARTS

a limited scale continues near Horseshoe Bay and The Neck.

The Neck was the focus of European settlement in the years leading up to the 1840 signing of the Treaty of Waitangi and colonisation. Historian Basil Howard, reviewing the sealing and whaling eras, says The Neck attracted 'a motley gathering of seafarers from foc's'le and quarter-deck'. They were mostly British, but a few were Spanish, Portuguese, Australian and American. They settled among the Maori at The Neck, took Maori wives, and paid for parcels of land with blankets, clothes, tobacco and cash, and sometimes with muskets, powder and balls.

When Bishop Selwyn, first Anglican Bishop of New Zealand, visited the island in 1844 he recorded the population at The Neck as: thirteen European men, all with Maori wives, and a total of fifty-six children. Around at Port William he found thirty Maori in residence. At Halfmoon Bay (today's Horseshoe Bay), where he conducted several marriages and baptisms, Selwyn described a domestic scene as he took shelter in the evening from rough weather:

> While I am writing 5 whalers are sitting at supper — I have just finished my rasher and pancake. Round the wood fire in a large open chimney 4 natives and 3 half-caste children also at supper. Dogs are prowling for scraps in the interstices. All looking very comfortable though the wind is howling and the rain pattering without. A blustering day; but some good, I hope, done. Little boy saying grace between his father's knees.

Under the Deed of Cession 1864, through which instrument the Government acquired the bulk of the island from the Rakiura Maori, The Neck was declared a Maori reserve. Reserves were also established at Lords River, Port Adventure, Ohekia (Paterson Inlet), Horseshoe Bay, Port William, Ruggedy River, Mason Bay (South Head), Port Easy and Southern Titi Islands.

Closure of The Neck to further European settlement meant that new colonists had to look elsewhere. They looked to Halfmoon Bay, whose Maori name, Kai-rakau, probably referred to edible produce of the forest. In 1864, the bay was uninhabited. The following year, the first European settler moved in, and by 1870 a small village had been established.

The first post office, designated 'Stewart's Island', was strategically sited on Ulva Island in the middle of Paterson Inlet, halfway between the new village and the old settlement of The Neck. Charles Traill, the first postmaster, who ran a store on Ulva, would hoist a flag to signal the arrival of mail, and residents would boat over from The Neck, Halfmoon Bay and the sawmilling settlements dotted along the northern shores of Paterson Inlet. Timber, growing right to the shoreline of Paterson Inlet and around the coast, was a major drawcard for settlers, and boatbuilding a worthy end-use.

The Neck School (1875–88). Arthur Traill, standing in the doorway, was the first teacher. A school inspector, Mr Pope, is with the main group of pupils. The photograph was probably taken in the early 1880s
Rakiura Museum

STEWART ISLAND

Trampers Simon and Paula Marwick negotiate the Chocolate Swamp on the way to Mason Bay

THE SETTLED PARTS

Hunters loading deer at Mason Bay

But the provincial authorities at Invercargill continued to dream of a major colony based on farming and fishing and assisted immigration — Scottish immigrants preferred. In April 1873, a group of twenty-four Shetland Islanders — five families and two single men — landed at Port William, where barracks accommodation for 150 had been built. Within a year the settlement had been abandoned. By all accounts the newcomers were demoralised by the lack of a profitable market for their fish, and no doubt isolation was a factor as well. Today, the only outward signs of the existence of the Port William Special Settlement of the 1870s are clumps of exotic trees and shrubs.

Officialdom's choice of Port William over, say, Halfmoon or Horseshoe Bays is intriguing. It might have had its origins in the days of sail, for full-rigged ships would have manoeuvred more easily in Port William than in the next two harbours south, which present sailing vessels with awkward head winds in a sou'wester.

Port William, named after an early Sydney shipowner, was an important base for sealers working the Foveaux grounds in the first decade of the nineteenth century. As to the question of which sealers' base became the first European settlement south of Foveaux Strait, Codfish Island stakes a claim — coincidentally, the Newfoundland (Whenuahou) of the southern Maori people. During the revival of the sealing trade in the mid-1820s, sealers established a small settlement at Sealers Bay, a sandy beach on the north-east side of the island, the lee shore. Wrote Basil Howard:

> In view of the lack of evidence, traditional and documentary, the historian can say little more than that about 1825 sealers living on Codfish Island took Maori wives and founded the first permanent settlement south of Foveaux Strait . . . the first true settlers in Stewart Island.

Codfish Island never developed as a settlement. It did not appeal to the whalers who followed the sealers into these waters, its timber supplies were limited, and the peaty soil was unsuitable for agriculture. By 1850 it was deserted, overtaken by newer settlements on the main island.

Another settlement that also did not progress was founded at Port Pegasus in 1826 by a party of colonists from the Bay of Islands in the far north of New Zealand. Shipbuilding was their purpose. Led by an English shipbuilder, William Cook, the party included seven shipwrights and sawyers. Cook had a Maori wife with him. They had been told of the rosy prospects in the deep south by one William Stewart — Stewart the sealer it seems, posing as the namesake who drew the chart of Pegasus. Within a few months Stewart had left the colonists to their own devices. They set about building a schooner (which, it is thought, was bought by a Sydney merchant, George Weller, and named the *Joseph Weller*) but ended up with a reputation as whaleboat builders. Cooks Arm in Port Pegasus is no doubt named after the leader of the group — not James Cook.

Sealer-adventurer John Boultbee called at Pegasus in 1827 and left this interesting portrait of life there:

An artist's impression of life in a sealers' camp about 1810
Edmund Farr, *Voyages*, Alexander Turnbull Library

The men looked lean and haggard, but the women stood hunger well, and the fernroot seemed to keep them in as plump a condition as if they had the best food to live upon. It is remarkable how the New Zealanders can stand hunger; I have seen them for 2 days with scarcely anything to eat; and still retain their good humour. Not so the Europeans, they invariably grow clamorous and quarrelsome.

The Pegasus shipbuilders left little evidence of their industry, besides a few mud-covered keel supports and jetty piles. By 1840, when HMS *Herald* called to declare British sovereignty over the island, Port Pegasus was deserted.

*

Fishing and tin mining brought people back to live at Pegasus from the turn of the century through to the 1930s, but when the focus of the fishing industry switched to Halfmoon Bay and the minerals ran out, settlement was doomed. It was impossibly hard for anyone to live off the land, so poor in quality were the soils.

The tin-mining boom lasted two years — 1888 to 1890. It followed the discovery of cassiterite, and thus stream tin, in the Pegasus Creek area of North Arm. By December 1888, forty-one prospecting licences had been issued, heralding a full-blown search for the parent lode. Services arrived in the form of a store and post office, but by early 1890 the rush was over.

Gold prospectors fared no better — a flurry of interest here and there, starting in 1867 with the discovery of fines just south of Magnetic Beach, Port William. But no one was going to get rich. Quartz reefs in the Ruggedy Mountains excited interest until companies formed to work them announced the prospect fruitless. The island's true riches lay in the sea, as generations of Maori nomads knew.

And just as Maori fishers had cured their fish to preserve them, so too did the early Pakeha settlers — until refrigeration became available in the 1890s. In 1862, a trader and boatbuilder, Captain James Harrold, sent samples of dried, salted and smoked fish to Invercargill and Dunedin from his fish-

Harrolds Bay, where Captain James Harrold ran a small boatyard in the 1860s. The stone cottage was built in the 1830s by Lewis Acker
Rakiura Museum

curing station at Port William. Harrold went on to establish a boatyard at the bay on Ackers Point Peninsula that bears his name. He occupied the old stone cottage of Lewis Acker, American whaleman and later shipowner, which is still to be seen at Harrolds Bay — the island's oldest building still standing. Stone for it was brought over from New River estuary near Invercargill as ship ballast.

In the 1870s, Charles Traill, the Ulva settler who was a noted botanist and conchologist, experimented with tinning oysters, fish and crayfish. Regular shipments of fresh fish to Bluff began in 1885 with the establishment of a weekly steamer service, and the advent of refrigeration in the next decade enabled the fishing industry to develop fully. The first refrigeration plant was set up at Port Pegasus in 1897. Halfmoon Bay became the fishing industry's main base in 1920

STEWART ISLAND

Fisherman Steven Firestone prepares gear for the crayfishing season

Colin Neighbours filleting blue cod

Boatshed

STEWART ISLAND

Fishing station, Thomson's Jetty, Port Pegasus, 1915. The ketch *Rakiura* is at the wharf Rakiura Museum

Whalers' base, Kaipipi, Paterson Inlet. Whale catchers of a Norwegian company overwintered at this sheltered bay in the 1930s
George M. Turner, Rakiura Museum

when the Stewart Island Fishing Company installed a freezer there.

Commercial species included blue cod, groper, trumpeter, moki and greenbone, with cod and groper mainstays of the industry. The trade in crayfish did not flourish until after the Second World War. Oysters are not recognised today as distinctively Stewart Island in origin, but around the period of colonisation the island was renowned for its oyster stocks.

Oysters, or tio, figured in the pre-European Maori diet. Port Adventure had particularly rich pickings, which the Pakeha soon learned about. In 1830, the brig *Argo* arrived at Sydney laden with produce from southern New Zealand: flax, potatoes, pigs, wheat, and thirty jars of Port Adventure oysters. The exploitation that followed was so ruthless the Government closed the beds in 1872. Port William was another place where oysters thrived, but the beds there were similarly thrashed.

Earlier in the century, whalemen hunted the biggest 'fish' in the sea, heedless of how many they were taking and the impact on stocks. Mostly of American and Australian nationality, they hunted sperm and southern right whales in southern seas and tended to base their operations at South Island harbours rather than at Stewart Island. When Southern Ocean whaling was revived in the 1920s, a Norwegian company chose a bay called Kaipipi (Prices) as a winter-over base. Small, steam-powered chaser boats were overhauled there while the mother ship returned to Norway. Relics of that industry lie scattered in Kaipipi today.

Kaipipi, on the north side of Paterson Inlet, also features in the history of sawmilling on the island. Two mills, one steam-driven, the other powered by waterwheel, were set up at Kaipipi in 1861. Although timber looked to be a promising industry for the island, with resources as far as the eye could see, it turned out to be limited by market realities. Local shipwrights and carpenters could utilise only so much; the rest had to be exported across the strait, and that somewhat larger island had ample supplies of its own. There were never more than four mills operating at any one time on Stewart Island. Most were located on the northern shores of Paterson Inlet or around Halfmoon Bay.

As more and more land was gazetted nature or scenic reserve, and the competitive edge disappeared in freight costs, the sawmilling quietly packed up. The last mill in operation, at Maori Beach, Port William, closed in 1931. Its boiler lies rusting in the dunes.

In the seventy years to 1931, the loggers cut an estimated 2,500 hectares of forest — the most accessible and desirable stands, of course, but in reality only the fringes of the resource, which is substantially protected today.

It takes a trained eye to see where the loggers worked; the forest is striking back. In places the canopy features same-age stands of kamahi, evidence of clear-fell, but the bigger and slower-growing rimu are represented as seedlings, saplings and pole-sized trees, and they will come to dominate again.

Old cobbers: Messrs A. Ford and J. Hay lived alone at Port Pegasus in houses a few yards apart during the latter part of last century. Mr Ford is holding a cat, the forerunner of many a wild cat perhaps
Rakiura Museum

Murdoch's sawmill, Horseshoe Bay, around the turn of the century
Rakiura Museum

Of all the island's resources and assets of value to humans, there is one that has stood the test of time — the muttonbird. Seasonal and sustainable muttonbirding was a primary reason for Maori occupation of the island.

Around October each year, the titi migrate in their millions to southern islands to breed after wintering in the North Pacific. Mostly they return to small offshore islands, including the clusters near Rakiura's south-west and north-east coastline — the Titi Islands. For centuries, Maori have travelled to these islands in March–April for the ritual harvest of the young of the titi.

When the adult birds stop feeding their single chick about the beginning of April, the harvest begins. In the first few weeks the young birds are pulled from the burrows and quickly killed by a blow from a heavy stick or a wringing of the neck; later, when they are venturing from their burrows at night, the hunting is done by torchlight. In the old days, torches were

STEWART ISLAND

Westerly gale on Paterson Inlet

THE SETTLED PARTS

Sunrise over Ackers Point lighthouse

Muttonbirders' kelp bags hanging out to dry, Braggs Bay
Rakiura Museum

made from totara bark lashed with flax fronds and soaked in muttonbird fat.

The process of preserving the birds involved cooking and packing them in their own fat — salt is the preserving agent today — in pouches (poha) made from the leathery bull kelp, or rimurapa. Strips of totara bark, forming a protective sheath, were tied around the kelp bags. Making the poha was a specialised task in itself. Blades of kelp were carefully selected for the purpose, blown up using the hollow stems of the punui plant (*Stilbocarpa lyallii*) and hung out to dry for a few weeks.

Muttonbirding was singled out in the 1864 Deed of Cession as an unalienable right of the Rakiura Maori and their descendants, and it is a tribute to the strength of the tradition that it should be so enshrined when elsewhere most Maori practices associated with mahikakai (food gathering and food resources) were trampled on by colonisation and given no legal recognition. The Deed allowed the Rakiura Maori free access to the Southern Titi Islands, some twenty-one in all. But it cast the northern islands, lying in the strait between Rakiura and Ruapuke, into Crown ownership — a contentious decision, as the muttonbirders must apply for permits to take titi there.

Today, muttonbirding is principally a commercial activity, serving markets, although no one can deny it reinforces the Maori identity of the participants and adds both adventure and a communal dimension to their lives. Instead of landing from boats — at some personal risk if the seas are high — many now choose to get to and from family birding grounds by helicopter. The season runs from 1 April to 31 May — two hectic months. Annual takes in recent generations have been estimated to go as high as 300,000 birds.

The name muttonbird probably originated in Australia, where the flesh of the young titi was likened to sheepmeat, and where, in Tasmania at least, the Aborigines also developed a taste for it in ancient times. Muttonbird — the very name can make the mouth water if the mouth belongs to a titi connoisseur. Not everyone would agree, though. The *Acheron* journal, of 1850, had this to say about titi:

They are the most disgusting objects, with a rank, rammish odour sufficient to deter any but the coarsest appetites.

Between seasons the modern muttonbirding camps are usually deserted. They represent settlement of a sort — the only Maori encampments to survive on Rakiura. The settlements of old have gone the way of all organic matter in a moist climate. Settlement sites exhibit only postholes, occasional stone-working and butchery areas, stone artefacts and kitchen middens of shell and bone. What the houses looked like can only be guessed at, although John Boultbee, who lived amongst the Fiordland and Foveaux Strait Maori for just on two years (1826–28), described the houses in fashion in the south at the time. Of single gable and high-roof design, they were made of totara bark cladding and combinations of manuka and toetoe stems, supplejack, raupo and plaited flax. The inhabitants, according to Boultbee, slept on 'elevated platforms about 3 feet from the ground' and they would sit on these platforms to do handwork such as mat-making. There was provision for a fireplace at one end.

Thirty years after Boultbee's visit, a village was established at Port Adventure in the strangest circumstances. The new settlers were escaping the rigours of a sub-Antarctic climate. They had gone to the Auckland Islands in the 1840s —Maori refugees and their Moriori slaves from the Chatham Islands — and now remnants of that community were trying their luck on milder Rakiura, even if it did constitute another tribe's patch and they could therefore claim no rights or mana over the land. In the event, the Port Adventure settlement lasted only a few years. But the climate was definitely kinder to them — they grew potatoes on sections hacked out of the bush — as it was for the Rakiura Maori who preceded them. Charles Traill would comment in later years:

> The natives assure me that peaches used to ripen in their pleasantly situated gardens at Port Adventure.

Land reserved for the Rakiura Maori is located mainly in the

Roadworks, Halfmoon Bay, in the 1880s
Rakiura Museum

STEWART ISLAND

The first wharf at Halfmoon Bay, 1879. A smokehouse for curing fish is behind the wharf building   Rakiura Museum

north-east sector of the island, north of Lords River. The Neck is the focal point of Maori sentimental interest. Although few people live there today, its long-standing use for settlement and for farming can be seen in the amount of land given over to pasture and scrub that must have once been tall forest.

*

Halfmoon Bay, capital of the island, has won back a fair amount of bush that was cleared a century ago. In addition, it has acquired some significant introduced vegetation, like the elegant eucalyptus trees (blue gums) lining the waterfront at Lonnekers and various native trees that are rare or missing altogether from the island flora — trees such as lemonwood (tarata), kowhai and mahoe that add colour and scent to the bush locally. Ironically, a few distinctively Stewart Island species survive around Halfmoon Bay and adjacent settled areas because of the protection afforded from browsing animals. A notable example of this is the big-leafed Stilbocarpa herb, punui, which is very palatable to deer and quickly eaten out. Although closely related to a South Island congener, this species is found only on Stewart and Solander Islands.

Not only do a few certain uncommon native plants flourish in the vicinity of Halfmoon Bay, certain native birds are at home here, too. Kaka, the forest parrots, make screeching treetop-to-treetop flights over the village, especially around sunset when their underwing feathers flash a deep-red hue. Nectar-feeding tui, their wings whirring urgently, will dash about the place all day in defence of territory, displaying an aggression quite out of character with their liquid melodies. Native pigeons are always bending branches with their plumpness as they search for berries and other tasty things. On the forested margins of settlement, a few flightless weka can still be seen going about their woodhen business in broad daylight. Out on Ackers Point Peninsula and in bays quite close to roads and houses, the burrowing blue penguins, or korora, get busy in the evenings.

The presence of these and other native birds in and around the built-up areas is a satisfying sign that, given not too many hazards and hindrances, the wild will come to town.

STEWART ISLAND

Exposed coastal vegetation

THREE

Coast to Coast

Often the most enduring images of an island are of its coastline. Maybe this is because there is no more dynamic place on earth than the seashore — a sibilant seam marking off terrestrial life from marine life; never the same, never still. Stewart Island's shores pulse with life.

On the terrestrial side of the seam, right around the island, tree daisies give the vegetation a distinctive appearance, forming tight canopies on exposed bluffs where the going is too tough for bigger trees. They tolerate the frontline positions, closest to the tide.

These are the trees of the Stewart Island's famous muttonbird scrub, so named because they cover the breeding grounds of titi, the sooty shearwater, on the offshore islands. *Brachyglottis rotundifolia* (puheretaiko) is the species usually identified as muttonbird scrub, but the term can apply to other tree daisies, notably *Olearia colensoi* (tupare, sometimes called leatherwood), and *Olearia oporina* (teteaweka), which has eye-catching flowers — white-edged with deep-purple centres. Teteaweka is not scared of heights. It climbs to 400 metres on the Ruggedy Range.

To survive dehydrating winds and salt spray, tree daisies are equipped with leaves as thick as leather. In some species the texture underneath is felt-like. Their seeds are fluffy and disperse in the wind, hence the species' colonising ability.

On sheltered and relatively fertile sites, the muttonbird scrub is overtopped by rimu, rata and kamahi, which show their appreciation at the most favourable sites by overhanging the sea.

Sharing frontline status on the coast with the tree daisies is another shrub — the grasstree, or inaka, *Dracophyllum longifolium*, whose range on Stewart Island extends from the shoreline to the sub-alpine zone. The mountain flax, *Phormium cookianum*, named after Captain Cook, is another plant that lives both at the coast and at altitude. Coastal specialists include the shrub, *Hebe elliptica* (kokomuka), a native also of southern South America, and the Stewart Island forget-me-not, *Myosotis rakiura*, which is found only in southern New Zealand, decorating banks and cliffs in summer with clusters of white flowers, classically forget-me-not in style.

Once common on the main island, but confined now to the small islands free of introduced mammals, is Cook's scurvy grass, *Lepidium oleraceum*, a lush herb growing to about half a metre in height. Browsing animals are partial to its glossy green leaves. So, apparently, were Captain Cook's crew. Tasting of cabbage, the leaves were collected for their antiscorbutic properties, although not from Stewart Island, as the *Endeavour* did not land here. The lepidium and wild celery, *Apium prostratum*, were equally sought after — '. . . as much

STEWART ISLAND

Olearia oporina

Ruggedy coastline

Sellery and Scurvy grass as loaded the boat,' wrote Cook. *Apium*'s alternative common name, shore parsley, also hints of culinary potential.

For most of its broken length the coastline is rocky. On the west coast the extent of wave erosion is typical of southern oceanic islands, and the vegetation there feels the wind acutely. Coastal shrubs and trees bow to windshear; in the most terrible storms patches of them will collapse.

The impact of the wind is graphically portrayed wherever dunes occur on the west coast — at Doughboy Bay, Mason Bay and the Hellfire and Ruggedy Beaches at the northern end. The wind-driven sand eats its way inland, devouring coastal forest in its dune-building. Plant life adopts clever strategies to combat these conditions.

At the frontline of plant life on sandy shores is an orange-tufted sedge called pingao, *Desmoschoenus spiralis*, which creates habitat for itself by binding the sand with rope-like rhizomes — row upon row. Pingao used to adorn beaches from North Cape to Rakiura and was coveted by Maori weavers. It is on the threatened species list today, surviving only where it is not outmanoeuvred and overwhelmed by introduced marram grass.

Marram, tall, tussocky and quick-spreading, was planted at Mason Bay early this century to stabilise the sand, but its seeds will travel by sea. Marram has established itself in the past on Codfish Island dunes.

Only on remoter parts of mainland New Zealand — notably Stewart Island — does pingao grow plentifully. It is a botanical treasure, occupying a genus of its own; in other words, it has no near relatives anywhere in the world — a sign of a long, isolated ancestry. Pingao has presided over eons of dune-building and shoreline change.

*

The most recent rise in sea levels, going back some 5,000 years, has created a shoreline at Stewart Island about as varied in nature as it is possible to get, based on rock, sand and mud-flat — hard shores and soft. The contrast between the west and east coasts is greatest along a line of latitude linking Mason Bay with Paterson Inlet and its outer shores. This is where the sea makes its strongest bid to split Stewart Island in half. Paterson Inlet extends so far west that the upper reaches of South West Arm are just thirteen kilometres in a direct line from the ocean at Mason Bay, and the near-flat walk from tidal Freshwater River to the bay can be done in just three or four hours. Although controlled by the same sea, these shores are worlds apart in character.

Mason Bay's thirteen-kilometre arc of sand, expansive dunelands and broad seascape excite wild and poetic thoughts. Herbert Guthrie-Smith, a naturalist and gentleman farmer from Hawke's Bay, wrote about Mason Bay after a visit in 1911:

> Westward lies an alien continent across vast water solitudes, eastward dry dunes, the playground of the wind. Blown sand, clear seas, heaven's vault above, and space illimitable, these are the features of the bay.

Scientific imagination has been stirred, too, by the bay's strange landscape. In the 1970s, geologists investigated a theory that Mason Bay had extraterrestrial origins — that it was formed by the impact of a meteorite. There were questions to answer: Could the smooth curve of sand be part of a huge drowned crater? And were the odd-looking rock outcrops in the dunes not shatter cones so typical of meteorite strikes?

Apparently not. The geologists concluded the outcrops had been created by the force and sand-blasting effect of the westerly winds. Still, contradiction of the meteorite theory takes nothing away from the look of those rocks. The place is unearthly. Aeolian — from Aeolus, the Greek god of wind — is how the geologists describe the dunefield. The Mason Bay dunefield extends inland for three kilometres and climbs to 150 metres above sea level. The older dunes are claimed by rata forest, which has pingao to thank for staking the claim several hundred years earlier.

Inland of the active dunes, the Mason Bay flats spread east

to the foot of a green wall of hills, the Rakeahua Range. It is easy to see how this country would have enticed pastoralists. It contains fourteen square kilometres of tussock grassland readily accessible from the beach, and at the south end of the beach, within the sheltering crook of the Ernest Islands, farm supplies can be landed and wool shipped out. The feature plant of the flats is the magnificent red tussock.

Red tussock, *Chionochloa rubra*, whose leaves shine with a rich rufous or copper colour when the sun is low, grows to a metre or more in height. Two-thirds of the island's red tussock resource is found on the Mason Bay plains, where it is close to its southern limits. On wetter sites it is joined by manuka, inaka and the common New Zealand flax, *Phormium tenax*, and usually overtops the swamp umbrella fern, *Gleichenia dicarpa* and dense springy mats of wire rush, *Empodisma minus*, known also as tanglefoot.

Sheep farming knocked back much of the red tussock, but it is recovering quickly following the removal of the sheep. In a quaint juxtaposition of new and old fauna, sheep used to graze alongside kiwis probing the sandy soils around the tussocks for worms, beetles and other invertebrates. Now the kiwis have the place to themselves. Because of the low, open nature of its vegetation, Mason Bay is known for its kiwi-spotting potential. Here the birds are liable to emerge from their burrows in the daytime to feed. One bird used to whistle its presence around noon. So much for the nocturnal and secretive reputation of New Zealand's national bird!

Some kiwi territories incorporate the high dunes, where bold footprints will show out in the sand until obliterated by the next bout of wind. A kiwi track in the sand is a distinctive trademark of Mason Bay. Leonard Cockayne, in 1909, noted other mementos:

> . . . here the southern ocean, unchecked for thousands of miles, strikes from the west with the full power of its might. Nor come the waters altogether empty-handed. Many strange offerings lie upon the glistening sands — the precious and perfume-bearing ambergris, pumice from the volcanic region of the north, curious shells and trees, too, not of Stewart Island.

The debris today is not always natural. It includes a frightening amount of fishing paraphernalia, virtually all of it plastic and incapable of being digested by the land — plastic bottles, buckets, baskets and floats plus rope, strapping and bits of net. There is a small bay at the south end of Mason Bay, just south of a neck of sand joining the Ernest Islands to the main island, where the marine debris accumulates in absurd quantities. On the same beach Maori middens are eroding from low dunes — the rubbish of a subsistence culture mixing with the rubbish of a careless, if not ruinous, one.

But to return to Cockayne's observations: he made an interesting point about trees 'not of Stewart Island' washing up. He was referring, one imagines, to the logs of exotic species. But the sea carries more than logs; it is a seed-dispersal mechanism.

Marram grass has migrated this way. So too has kowhai, although its seeds rarely get beyond the germination stage before being washed away by high seas. Kowhai has not been able to recolonise the island after the ice ages, as its bright yellow seeds, though hardy and buoyant, cannot disperse upstream or uphill. The kowhai trees around Halfmoon Bay have had a helping hand from humans.

*

Due east of Mason Bay and the Rakeahua Range is a shoreline strikingly different in character from the weather coast of the island — Paterson Inlet. In the inlet's upper reaches, the sea mingles with fresh water and, bereft of swell, merely laps the banks at high tide. The ebb tide, timid, leaves huge areas of mud exposed. Here is the island's most extensive estuarine system.

Estuaries on this scale elsewhere in the country are often modified and trampled on by human creations such as rubbish dumps, sewage outfalls, port development, dredging and reclamation. Estuarine life at the head of Paterson Inlet goes on

STEWART ISLAND

Clumps of *Carex secta* in waterlogged areas behind sand dunes

Eroded cliffs, Mason Bay

The native sand binder, pingao

Dunes are ever-changing under the influence of wind

more or less unmolested. The shellbanks — sinuous ribbons of empty cockle shells extending hundreds of metres — hint of the scale of productivity here. The cockles, filter-feeders, are preyed on by oystercatchers, which use their sabre-like bills to prise out the fish. They can eat a couple of hundred a day. Other cockles fall prey to whelks, univalve shellfish that scent food with a siphon resembling, in miniature, a swinging elephant's trunk. The whelks tackle their prey in convincing style, boring small holes through the shells of other molluscs with apparatus called radula.

But plants contribute the basic energy to the estuary, and a pre-eminent species on the fringes is the jointed rush, *Leptocarpus similis*. It grows in clumps and dense stands that sway and shiver in the wind or when waves wash through them. The Maori name for this rush is oioi — to shake. Standing at the edge of sea and land, it seems to draw colours from both — shades of grey, green and blue, brownish purple and ochre. How the rush is going to look on any one day depends largely on the quality of the light.

As the stems of the jointed rush die and decay, they are colonised by tiny creatures that feed snails, worms, crabs and shrimps, some of which sustain fish. Flounder, yellow-eyed mullet, eels and galaxiids (including whitebait) frequent the shallows; and rig and spiny dogfish, two small species of shark, are thought to spawn in this habitat.

Containing salt-tolerant sedges, grasses and creeping herbs, saltmarsh forms the landward link with the woody vegetation; in the other direction lies a zone of vegetation that lives half the time immersed in the tide and half out of it. Dark-green meadows of eelgrass or seagrass (*Zostera novazelandica*) lie flat on the mud when the tide is out, sometimes mixed with Ulva sea lettuce, a bright green algae with wide, almost see-through leaves. The latter is edible but not as coveted by Maori as karengo (*Porphyra columbina*), which has a similar form but is purplish, grows on tidal rocks and rips less easily.

Despite the extent of silt and sand in the tidal flats, the waters of Paterson Inlet are relatively free of sediment. Very

Wetland habitat

Forest fallen victim to wind-driven sand

little comes down the rivers and streams, testimony to the intact state of the forest. This clarity of inshore waters is a hallmark of the Stewart Island coast in general and Paterson Inlet in particular.

The inlet has 190 kilometres of coastline, much of it rocky. In places, gravel or sand beaches soften the shoreline. At the entrance by The Neck the water is forty-five metres deep, but over most of the inlet the depths are in the order of fifteen to twenty-five metres. On still days the bottom may be visible through ten metres of water. The inlet contains more than twenty islands, the largest being four-kilometre-long Ulva, which contributes to the inlet's sheltered nature by blunting easterly swells.

The inlet is Seaweed City. It harbours seventy per cent of the island's 380 known seaweeds, red and brown. Meadows of red algae occupy large areas, although across much of the inlet the bottom is covered by sand and mud. Around the edges the underwater habitat is often rocky. Algae, sand, rock, and sheltered sea — a recipe for a breathtaking animal soup.

The underwater world of Paterson Inlet is filled with animals of fantastic shape and function. The less well known include sand-sifting sea cucumbers, tubeworms that build reefs of limestone as colourful as any tropical reef, and anemones, the size of dinner plates, which sting passing prey. There are sponges that strain their food, small white urchins called sea mice that bury themselves in the sand, and minute bryozoa that amalgamate their horny cases to form coral-like branches. Bryozoa attach themselves to rocks, anchored shellfish and even blades of seaweed.

Then there are the grazers of algae on subtidal reefs. These include kina, limpet, topshell, brittlestar, chiton and paua — the large blackfoot paua, *Haliotis iris*, and the yellowfoot, *Haliotis australis*. Starfish come in many forms. The larger ones stalk scallops on the mud bottom. But a succulent meal is not guaranteed, as the scallop can escape groping tentacles with a sudden convulsive flapping of its shell that will propel it away in a cloud of sediment.

Bull kelp

Dune lake

STEWART ISLAND

Granite rocks, west Ruggedy Beach

The tidal flats of Cooks Arm, Port Pegasus. The Fraser Peaks are in the background

STEWART ISLAND

Maori midden site

For shellfish design that has stood the test of time, none can match the brachiopods. Known also as lamp shells or mermaids' toenails, these bivalves are considered the world's oldest living animals. Their fossil history can be traced back 600 million years.

Paterson Inlet has four species, Port Pegasus five. What is significant about the Paterson Inlet brachiopods is their concentration — hundreds per square metre in places, just as in ancient times when brachiopods were dominant sea-floor animals in many parts of the world. They are filter-feeders, usually attached to rock or something solid by a tough stalk.

However, some species in Stewart Island waters have taken on a free-lying habit; thus they can be seen out in the middle of the inlet as well as around the rocky shore — a sign of sediment-free water. One free-lying species is *Neothyris lenticularis*, which has a smooth, pink, relatively large shell. Another is *Terebratella sanguinea*, red and fluted. The black *Notosaria nigricans* lives on rock walls as shallow as two metres.

All these species are common and occur in Foveaux Strait and Fiordland as well as Stewart Island. The shells of spent brachiopods often wash ashore, decorating beaches and shellbanks with black, red and pink 'toenails'.

Of international interest, the brachiopods can shed light on evolutionary history as a result of their prominence and continuity in the fossil record. They constitute not a family or even an order of animals, but a whole phylum — Brachiopoda. Their common name, lamp shell, refers to the stalk hole in the shell, reminiscent of the wick hole in old-style lamps.

The silty floor of Paterson Inlet is certainly no desert. Shellfish such as brachiopods, scallops and oysters are only a part of the food web. This is also the habitat of opalfish, flounder and other fish. Indeed, the inlet is renowned for its fish stocks.

The commonest fish is probably the spotty, a member of the wrasse family, which is common also in coastal waters. It has a few relatives here — banded wrasse and girdled wrasse, the latter peculiar to the colder southern waters of New Zealand.

Distinctive among the reef fish are blue moki, blue cod and the schooling trumpeter, all of which thrive in colder seas. Blue moki feed on worms and starfish. Blue cod is the best known. A long-lived fish (twelve years plus), it has a long tapering body, greenish-blue above, and grows to over sixty centimetres in length.

With crayfish and paua, blue cod is a mainstay of the island's fishing industry. Crayfish and paua were both once much more abundant in the inlet than they are today. Local people remember when paua used to lie as thick as cobblestones, and when crayfish could be caught in number right up the inlet. Near North Arm is a spot nicknamed 'Crayfish Village'.

In the outer areas of the inlet, among the algae forests, reef fish such as greenbone and leatherjacket join the blue moki and trumpeter. A quick-growing seaweed, bladder kelp (*Macrocystis pyrifera*), is common in the shallower water, where it can capitalise on the sunlight. Inshore, in sheltered bays, lives

Gunnera hamiltonii

Dolphins are regular visitors to Paterson Inlet

the intriguing Neptune's necklace (*Hormosira banksii*). Its strings of edible olive-green beads, often exposed at low tide, have no holdfast.

Among the larger creatures entering Paterson Inlet are bottlenose dolphins and fur seals. The seals haul out on rocky islets off Ulva Island. Sharks enter, too. The carpet shark, harmless to humans, forages at night for shellfish and crabs. Yellow-eyed penguins nest on the Bravo group of islands, and blue penguins have burrows on many a shore. During the day groups of blue penguins are often seen on the surface, porpoising home or out to feeding grounds, or simply resting, duck-like, with their heads up.

*

Bull kelp (*Durvillaea antarctica*), anchored by stout holdfasts, adds a decorative touch to the rocky ocean shores. Like many of the fish that live around and amongst it, this giant seaweed is at home in colder waters, and its blades and leaves swirl in the waves like tresses in a fickle wind. In southern New Zealand, including Stewart Island, bull kelp is accompanied by a related species, *D. willana*, whose leaves branch in a more complex way. This species was named after Eileen Willa, a long-time resident of Halfmoon Bay, who took a keen interest in marine flora. Each kelp has its own niche on the shore. Individual plants do come unstuck, though, no matter how favourable their anchorage, when their holdfasts are weakened by the tunnelling activity of a variety of small burrowing animals, including slater-like isopods.

On the shoreline guarding Paterson Inlet, both kelps are found, with *D. willana* conspicuous on the seaward side of Native Island. Native Island's ocean coast, a more peaceful place than the coastline on the opposite side of the island, at Mason Bay, is a handy place to sample subtidal life. The island is at the entrance of Paterson Inlet, separated by a narrow channel from the mainland at Ringaringa. It holds the remains of several old Maori settlement sites — faded outlines in the sand.

Neptune's necklace

When the large kelp on Native Island is defeated by deepening waters, bladder kelp makes its contribution to the underwater forest amidst gardens of encrusting sponges, colonial ascidians and sea tulips. Deeper still, the bladder kelp is replaced by the prolific red algae. An encrusting algae called Lithothamnion 'paint' coats boulders and reefs below the low-tide mark, providing grazing grounds for paua and brittlestars. This, too, is the haunt of crayfish and blue cod. Bodies of water mix and clash here as the tide works the inlet, resupplying nutrients for the plant and animal communities. Near the entrance there is a current of about three knots.

It is a colourful, complex world under the sea, so aptly called inner space. On a coastline as varied and as little explored as Stewart Island's there are bound to be species galore awaiting discovery, animal and plant. In 1979, a new kind of sea slug, since named *Janolus ignis*, was reported from Lords River. What adds to Stewart Island's potential for new species is its mid-ocean location close to a convergence of sub-Antarctic and sub-tropical bodies of water.

Site of early Maori settlement, Native Island

STEWART ISLAND

Buller's mollymawk resting near The Neck

COAST TO COAST

Murray Beach on the more sheltered east coast

If the describing and naming of coastal species is incomplete, how much more study must be done to achieve a proper understanding of the way they interact — their ecology.

Andreas Reischek, an Austrian bird collector and taxidermist, was among the naturalists who coasted around the island last century and came away loaded with impressions of its novelty. In January 1888, Reischek joined the government vessel *Stella* on a voyage to New Zealand's sub-Antarctic islands to reprovision castaway depots. On her way south, the *Stella* put in to Lords River briefly, and Reischek explored upriver in a row boat. The birdlife amazed him. There were many waterfowl — paradise and grey ducks, and brown teal — and forest birds in abundance. He reported it all to the Auckland Institute later in the year:

> A small species of weka, not yet described, was caught peeping out between the rocks. Its plumage is rust red . . . Great numbers of kaka parrots were flying about, warning their mates of our approach . . . A full-grown young tui was not sufficiently on the alert, for we saw a quail-hawk [falcon] dart down on it, seize it in its talons, and bear it away to a secluded tree. I shot the hawk in the act of devouring its victim, and here is the specimen.

The *Stella* carried on to Port Pegasus, where Reischek saw a leopard seal fishing in kelp, and a 'yellow-headed penguin so seldom seen by collectors'. A sailor shot one on the shore, 'imagining it to be a wallaby!'

The collectors who come these days have to be content with taking home only images.

FOUR

Forest Tall

Stewart Island's forest features the southernmost native conifers in New Zealand. The tallest of them are kahikatea, or white pine, and rimu, the red pine — trees that impart stature and charisma to the New Zealand rainforest. They stand out. They have pedigree, too. Their ancestry can be traced back to the forests of the ancient southern continent of Gondwana, from which the islands of New Zealand originate. Ancestors of kahikatea lived 100 million years ago. At the time, Gondwanaland had not fully broken up; New Zealand and Australia were still attached.

As a result of this Gondwana connection, the New Zealand conifers, or podocarps, have relatives in Australia and as far away as South America. On Stewart Island most areas of tall forest were probably wiped out by periods of glaciation — the ice ages — during the past two million years. Very few woody species would have survived. But on the lands to the north there were places where the conifers and other trees hung on, awaiting a time when they could reassert themselves.

When the glacier ice began retreating 14,000 years ago, signalling the start of another warm spell, the forest returned to Stewart Island. Podocarps like rimu and kahikatea send forth seed mounted on little pedestals of fleshy fruit (podocarp means 'seed on a foot'). Sweet and coloured bright red, orange or yellow, the fruit is readily devoured, seed and all, by forest birds that unwittingly take on the role of seed dispersers. Thus do the podocarps island hop and cross mountains.

Owing to constraints of climate and soil quality, neither rimu nor kahikatea achieve on Stewart Island the height and bole size they are renowned for north of Foveaux Strait. Kahikatea, New Zealand's tallest native tree, grows to about thirty metres on Stewart Island, about half its maximum height up north, while rimu, which can attain forty metres on favourable northern sites, is doing well to get to twenty-five metres here.

Nonetheless, the biggest trees on Stewart Island are impressive. They cultivate a sense of maturity and life force — the oldest living things in the forest, capable of surviving 500 years, perhaps more. The older rimu have trunks over a metre in diameter, with grey-brown bark slowly peeling off in thick strips to expose ringed patterns underneath.

Rimu (*Dacrydium cupressinum*) is the predominant podocarp on Stewart Island. In north-east areas especially, it shows out above a dark canopy of kamahi and southern rata, recognisable not only by its superior height but also by its uneven crown of drooping, olive-green foliage. The biggest trees are often well spaced, as if territorial. Fruit appears on the female trees in autumn.

Maori used to collect the fruit to eat, and Captain Cook added another use. On his second voyage to New Zealand,

FOREST TALL

Forest canopy

Kahikatea

Cook described how he used rimu, which he termed spruce, in beer making:

> We at first made it of a decoction of the spruce leaves; but finding that this alone made the beer too astringent, we afterwards mixed with it an equal quantity of the tea plant [manuka] which partly destroyed the astringency of the other, and made the beer exceedingly palatable, and esteemed by every one on board.

The recipe called for three or four hours' boiling of young rimu and manuka branches and the addition of molasses, water and yeast.

As seedlings, rimu grace the forest floor with long, drooping fronds that stand out from the other vegetation, signalling their intention to rise above all when light allows. In areas cleared of rimu during the sawmilling era and now dominated by kamahi, the rimu seedlings are returning in force. One day the skyline will be theirs again.

Kahikatea (*Dacrydium dacrydioides*) prefers the river flats to the hills. Although this podocarp is often said to like wet soils, it is in fact selecting out the fertile alluvium, which often happens to lie close to the water table. Stewart Island's limited stocks of kahikatea are found north of the Rakeahua Valley. The densest stands are in the Freshwater Valley and its tributaries, especially those on the south side of Mount Anglem.

Grey-barked kahikatea, called white pine on account of its pale timber, develops a distinctive spire shape as a young tree. The crown is less shapely when the tree is fully mature. As with rimu, only the female tree bears seed and fruit. If not beaten to the draw by the birds, Maori would collect the tiny fruits in baskets — a time-consuming task — or simply pick a handful to use as a kind of chewing gum.

The podocarp story does not begin and end with the two giants, kahikatea and rimu. Totara and miro, although smaller in stature, are just about as abundant as rimu, with thin-bark totara, *Podocarpus hallii*, a close associate of kahikatea in the river valleys. Miro (*Prumnopitys ferruginea*) fruits in late autumn and winter — a large drupe, with a purple-pink skin and yellowish flesh. New Zealand pigeons gorge themselves on this fruit until they are too heavy and too groggy to fly. To humans, the berries taste of turpentine, but they can serve as an effective deodorant for sweaty trampers! Less common than miro and totara is matai, the black pine (*Prumnopitys taxifolia*), which grows mostly on alluvial soils with kahikatea.

Another podocarp, yellow silver pine (*Lepidothamnus intermedius*), comes into its own in the southern half of the island, reaching nine metres in height. In the more rigorous conditions of the south, where rimu and kamahi do not do as well, the hardy yellow silver pine competes strongly for a place in the canopy. The yellowish tinge to its foliage contributes an extra dimension to the mosaic of greens.

Rimu, more tolerant than kahikatea of poor site and soil conditions, will range as high as 500 metres above sea level on Stewart Island. At this altitude, though, the tree is stunted and cannot hope to become more than a shrub. To see the forest giant in this reduced form is both surprising and disillusioning. In good going, the podocarps are towers of strength, and on Stewart Island they are indisputably in command of the tall forest.

*

Beech trees, the podocarp family's age-old competitors on the two other main islands of New Zealand, have not re-established here. Glaciation is thought to be responsible for their absence. When the ice retreated, the island was colonised by the trees which had the most effective seed dispersal. Beech forest spreads only slowly.

According to fossil evidence there was once some beech forest on Stewart Island. Silver beech is the most cold-tolerant species, claiming the treeline in South Island subalpine areas, but the Stewart Island remnants were probably overrun by trees better adapted to a cool wet oceanic climate.

On the west coast of the South Island there is another 'beech gap' that is thought to be related to the ice-age history. This one runs for 150 kilometres between Greymouth and Paringa,

Totara forest

and the beech forest at either end is reinvading at a speed somewhat less than glacial.

The hardwoods that associate with rimu on Stewart Island — kamahai and southern rata — are flowering trees. They evolved much later than the podocarps. Kamahi (*Weinmannia racemosa*) produces its small white flowers on a stalk towards the end of the year. Lightly scented, the flowers turn reddish brown over summer, giving the canopy a rusty tinge. Southern rata (*Metrosideros umbellata*), in a good flowering year, will transform itself into a billowing red cloud. Its flowers are laden with nectar — sweet sustenance for tui, kaka and bellbird.

The dark-red heartwood of southern rata is very hard, hence its alternative common name, ironwood. Rata trunks tend to lean close to the ground in upland forest and on exposed ridges — a reaction to a stressful location. It is a habit seen also in the Auckland Islands, where the rata is at its southern limit.

Ferns, older in the evolutionary scale of things than any of the trees, add charm and filigree detail to the look of the forest. There are about eighty species of fern on the island, and any damp gully is bound to display a good range of them. They include several ferns named after their form or shape — kidney, umbrella, crown and Prince of Wales feather. The last mentioned (*Leptopteris superba*), bearing feathery deep-green fronds, was named for the ostrich plumes on the Prince of Wales' badge. The 'chickens' of the hen and chickens fern (*Asplenium bulbiferum*) are the tiny plants or bulbils that sprout along the length of the fronds and drop off to reproduce the parent vegetatively.

Many ferns have Maori names as well. One of the most distinctive species, the light-green umbrella fern *Sticherus cunninghamii*, reminded the Maori of the feet or footprints of the white heron, hence its name, waewae-kotuku.

Among the ferns of Stewart Island are four tree ferns, which, palm-like, add a tropical flavour to the rainforest. The commonest are the rough tree fern, or wheki, (*Dicksonia squarrosa*) and the black tree fern, or mamaku, (*Cyathea medullaris*), which is the tallest of them all. At up to ten metres high, the

Rata in flower

mamaku seems often to be challenging for a place in the canopy of the forest. The black trunk carries a distinctive hexagonal leaf-scar pattern. Its pith, baked, was a food of the Maori. Common in damp places throughout New Zealand, mamaku reaches its southern limit at Port Adventure.

The rough tree fern — trunk rough from broken-off old frond bases; fronds rough to touch — attains a height of about six metres. It has the habit, unlike other tree ferns, of producing new trunks from stolons that creep through the soil. Groves of wheki are often the result. It is also credited with an important role in forest regeneration.

The trunk of wheki, spiked with old frond bases, is an ideal vehicle for epiphytes. Many kamahi and rata trees begin life perched on the trunks of this tree fern, not to mention the broadleaf trees, coprosmas and five-finger Pseudopanax that also launch themselves this way. Their seeds lodge in moist crevices, germinate and take root. When the tree fern collapses, the woody species are grounded and able to grow into trees.

FOREST TALL

Umbrella fern

STEWART ISLAND

Manuka forest covers large areas of the Freshwater, Island Hill, Rakeahua and Toitoi Flats

FOREST TALL

Bush lawyer in flower

Save for climatic changes, this arrangement of flora worked undisturbed for eons. Then came deer.

Deer are partial to the young fronds of wheki. Although the tree fern remains fairly abundant, its stocks have been reduced, and by implication the regeneration of hardwood and other trees is affected. When natural regeneration is inhibited, the understorey trees thin out and the ground cover becomes the preserve of unpalatable plants — notably the crown fern, *Blechnum discolor*, and the hookgrass, *Uncinia uncinata*. Deer are not the only culprits. Possum browse on kamahi and rata leaves, causing dieback if sufficient damage is done.

Settlers brought deer to New Zealand for sport and possums for a trade in fur. Three European red deer were liberated in the Freshwater area in 1901, and eighteen American white-tailed, or Virginian, deer were put ashore at Port Pegasus in 1905. For a while they were protected, but by 1930 a ranger had been appointed with instructions to reduce their numbers.

Today, recreational hunters are encouraged to step up their hunting pressure on Stewart Island deer, especially the smaller and more numerous white-tailed. In north-west areas of the island, it has ravaged the understorey, creating a woodland effect out of coastal forest once lush and dense.

Broadleaft, or kapuka (*Griselinia littoralis*), a medium-sized tree with glossy leaves is a common target for deer, and its regeneration in places is at a standstill. Other forest species hit by deer and possum browsing include karamu (*Coprosma lucida*), kotukutuku (*Fuchsia excorticata*) and the small trees of the Pseudopanax group. Possums tend to gnaw the base of the Pseudopanax leaf stem, discarding the leaves in wasteful fashion. Where deer occur in number the hen and chickens fern is wiped out. Rats also affect regeneration, although to far less a degree. They consume the fruit and seed of many species, leaving telltale little heaps of drilled seed on the ground.

At one time pigs and goats roamed wild on Stewart Island, but they never established in any great number and finally disappeared — unlike the situation in the sub-Antarctic Auckland Islands, which had a problem with feral goats until an intensive

Ferns thrive in dark, damp gullies

culling programme in the late 1980s removed them. Wild pigs, however, continue to damage the natural biota of the main Auckland Island.

Forested gullies around Halfmoon Bay give an idea of what the lowland forest would look like without the deer and other animals. Species such as broadleaf, the semi-deciduous wineberry, or makomako, (*Aristotelia serrata*), pate (*Schefflera digitata*) and hen and chickens fern are reasonably common.

Wineberry, whose seed is bird-dispersed, is an early coloniser (with kotukutuku, manuka and kamahi) of lowland areas cleared by landslip or fire. Although the wineberry will initially outstrip the other colonisers, it eventually gives way to the kamahi or manuka.

Manuka (*Leptospermum scoparium*) can grow to extraordinary size, with trunks up to half a metre thick. On the more difficult sites, especially the wetter ones, it is not replaced by taller canopy species. It remains pre-eminent.

*

For all the damage done by the introduced mammals, the Stewart Island forest retains much of its natural character and forest associations. Mixtures of podocarp and hardwood forest cover almost two-thirds of the island; the remaining third is covered by low forest, shrubland, open grassland and herbfield.

The extent of forest cover is good news for the forest animal life. The bad news is that rats and cats range across the whole of it, making life hell for many species. More than a few have disappeared forever, perhaps even before science could register them in the book of life.

On the question of introduced predators, the only consolation is that the mustelid family — ferrets, stoats and weasels — have never become established in the wild on Stewart Island despite their notoriety in the South Island.

The forest birds that make Stewart Island special for visitors familiar with birdlife in northern forests are both members of the parrot family — kaka and kakariki, the parakeet.

FOREST TALL

Podocarp forest on alluvial soil features trees such as rimu, kahikatea and totara

The South Island kaka (*Nestor meridionalis meridionalis*) depends on large unbroken tracts of forest to sustain it. Much of its diet comprises insects and their larvae, especially wood-boring beetles, and it uses its powerful beak to tear off loose bark and excavate rotting timber in search of this food. Its numbers in South Island forests are thought to be dwindling, which makes the Stewart Island kaka community of vital conservation interest.

Well camouflaged in the forest, kaka are more often heard than seen in areas outside Halfmoon Bay. Their standard call is harsh and grating, but they can whistle, if the mood takes them, in a melodious way. Around Halfmoon Bay they take to the air in noisy flocks, especially at dusk and early in the morning — a sound-and-flight show.

Stewart Island is also a stronghold for a smaller distant relative of the kaka — the red-crowned parakeet (*Cyanoramphus novaezelandiae novaezelandiae*). Again, the intactness of the forest is a factor in their maintaining a good-sized population, for the species is scarce now on the larger islands to the north due to predation by stoats and rats, and loss of habitat. Yet it was so plentiful throughout the country in the 1880s, it was declared a public nuisance for raiding crops, orchards and gardens.

Like the kaka, kakariki (little kaka) will often choose a hollow in an old tree for a nest site. Its diet is just as varied as the kaka's — berries, seeds, young shoots, nectar and invertebrates. Its red forehead and crown distinguish it from the closely related yellow-crowned parakeet, which is in smaller numbers on Stewart Island. The two species live side by side on Ulva Island. In the North and South Island, for reasons not fully understood, the red-crowned is the rarer of the two. The voice of kakariki is not as raucous as that of kaka. Kaka screech parrot-fashion; kakariki keep up a rapid chatter, both in flight and while perching.

Leonard Cockayne reported the tui to be the 'commonest land bird' on Stewart Island in 1909, and its populations are still fairly high. The island at present also has good numbers of other well-known birds of the South Island forest — bellbird, grey warbler, yellow-breasted tit, brown creeper, silvereye and South Island fantail. The fantail is darker than its close cousin up north, and the black phase, as opposed to the common pied form, shows out more in the south.

Surprisingly, given its abundance in tall forest north of Foveaux Strait, the rifleman, New Zealand's smallest bird, is seldom encountered on Stewart Island.

One of the forest's most charming birds, the native robin, survives on Stewart Island. Identified as a subspecies (*Petroica australis rakiura*) as late as 1950, the Stewart Island robin is slightly smaller than the South Island bird, and darker in its upper plumage. It has the characteristic white breast of the New Zealand robin.

Sadly, for robin song adds cheer to any forest setting, this bird is now found in few places on the main island, although it is plentiful on several offshore islands. The Freshwater–Mason Bay area is probably the last place on Stewart Island where a sizeable population remains. Trampers on the Mason Bay track are almost guaranteed a close encounter of the robin kind somewhere in the manuka groves.

The robin, singly or in a small family group, will flit about near the ground and draw near if there is any suggestion the trampers are stirring up insect life. Its habit of observing things while braced almost at right angles on a vertical stem is a trademark of the long-legged robin. It also has a reputation for tameness.

Herbert Guthrie-Smith, the Hawke's Bay naturalist and gentleman farmer, wrote lyrically of many birds but for the robin he saved this gem:

> Sometimes I like to dream — 'tis but a vain imagining — that the exceeding trustfulness of the Robin may have evolved during some long gone golden age when mankind really loved his birds.

However tame-looking, the robin has exceptionally quick reflexes and is not going to fall victim to every wild cat that comes pouncing. Nonetheless, its numbers are greatly reduced since Leonard Cockayne undertook his vegetation surveys during the first decade of this century. Cockayne saw the robin at many locations but found it 'especially abundant in the neighbourhood of Port Pegasus', where few are seen today.

When a forest loses species — and the Stewart Island forest has lost birds within living memory, not to mention unique bats and certain kinds of lizard — it is the poorer. It is like losing a few cogs in a finely balanced wheel. The wheel still turns, but not quite as smoothly.

From the tiniest soil organism to the tallest podocarp, the forest is a living community of plants and animals. Despite its missing species, the Stewart Island forest remains intact enough to convey a community spirit.

FIVE

The High Ground

Stewart Island projects to visitors an image based on lush forest descending to the sea — an unbroken green backdrop to countless tranquil bays and beaches. There is no denying the power and appeal of this image, but it only partly represents the nature of the island.

To complete the picture it is necessary to travel to the land lying above 500 metres in altitude — alpine Stewart Island. Travelling there is easier said than done, of course. There are no roads; barely any tracks. And as for the weather, the rough days are likely to outnumber the fine two to one.

Here lies a world far removed from the intimate, balmy forest — a world bared to the elements, wind worried and hunkered down, and strangely, outlandishly beautiful. How odd to find such diverse form, colour and texture in the plant life of this world. How puzzling the idea that a climate and environment as spartan as this could support so many flowering species — daisies, buttercups and gentians, for example — and such varied foliage. Here in the highlands of Stewart Island is proof that plant life can excel in conditions inhospitable to humans.

The uplands in question comprise the Anglem massif at the northern end of the island, and to the south of Paterson Inlet, the Rakeahua Range, the Table Hill–Tin Range complex and the Deceit Peaks to the west of the Tin Range. These mountains represent ecological stepping stones between the temperate land masses to the north and the sub-Antarctic islands to the south.

Isolated for eons, the islands of New Zealand have a rich and distinctive collection of alpine plants that evolved through alternating periods of glaciation and warmth. Some of the plants are island endemics — species confined to one island or another. Stewart Island possesses several plants — and small animals — that are unique to it, reflecting a long enough period of insulation from the bigger islands for speciation to occur. To boast an array of endemics adds lustre to any island's identity.

A survey of Stewart Island's alpine flora published in 1992 identified twenty-one endemics. In other words, three-quarters of the plants unique to the island inhabit the alpine zone. Seven of them are restricted to Mount Anglem, and seven are found only on the southern ranges (Mount Rakeahua, Table Hill, Tin Range). This suggests that water once flowed between the northern and southern rangelands, isolating the two communities for long periods.

All three Acyphilla species — commonly called spaniard or speargrass — are endemic. Three Celmisia daisies and three Ranunculus buttercups are found nowhere else. The tussock grasses (snowgrasses) also have a local flavour. One of the five species or subspecies is endemic — the slender-leaved

Chionochloa lanea, found south of Table Hill — and another is an endemic subspecies, *C. crassiuscula crassiuscula*.

The tall forest does not rise to any great height on the island. The southern climate keeps the timberline low and indistinct. Tussock shrublands make their presence felt above the 500-metre contour in the north and the 300-metre mark in the south. Mountain leatherwood (*Olearia colensoi* var. *argentea*) is dominant in both areas. Common associates of it are manuka, inaka, mountain flax, and the tawny-green snow tussocks, *Chionochloa flavescens* in the north and *C. lanea* in the south.

The shrublands can be devilishly difficult to negotiate on foot. Botanist Thomas Kirk led a party of plant collectors up Mount Anglem in the 1880s and reported scrub 'so thick a retriever dog was unable to proceed'.

Yet today the most accessible part of the alpine zone, thanks to a well-defined track, is the area surrounding Mount Anglem, the island's highest peak at 980 metres, after an Irish whaler and pilot, Captain William Anglem, who settled at The Neck in 1842. From Halfmoon Bay, the summit is a three-day tramp (two days for the superfit). Anglem's summit ridge runs for about nine kilometres, and in summer it is lit up with flowers. Most species are white. They include the spectacular blooms of the mountain buttercup, *Ranunculus lyallii*; the delicate cups of the endemic Mount Anglem gentian, *Gentiana gibbsii*, which open only in full sunshine; and an endemic Celmisia species (resembling the South Island species *C. du rietzii* but more leathery of leaf) that presents its characteristic daisies on tall stalks.

Among the plants that add splashes of yellow to the scene is the bog lily, *Bulbinella gibbsii*, another endemic. It carries its flower head on stems up to thirty centimetres tall. As its common name suggests, it prefers wet ground, and in winter its orange-edged leaves die to ground level.

Around Mount Anglem and a neighbouring peak, Little Mount Anglem (738 metres), alpine plants create an attractive scene by their foliage alone. Shape, colour and texture vary enormously. Pineapple scrub, *Dracophylum menziesii*, holds up its reddish leaves in tufts resembling the tops of pineapples; the dwarf lily, *Astelia linearis*, sprouts stiff green leaves directly from the ground; the diminutive mountain daisy, *Celmisia clavata*, has short, whitish leaves that form tufted mats; the dwarf spaniard, *Aciphylla traillii*, forms its orange-green, sharp-pointed leaves into clumps; and the Stewart Island vegetable sheep, *Raoulia goyenii*, produces a greenish-white hummock up to about a metre across, which Leonard Cockayne described as looking 'more like a clump of coral than a living plant'.

The Raoulia is one of the curious cushion plants. Compact, ground-hugging and often rounded, it covers extensive areas of the alpine zone. Its leaves are tightly pressed, its branches absurdly short. It is a survivor, having evolved this form to combat the conditions, especially the bitter winds. Decaying leaves form a layer of peat beneath the plant — its nutrient bank and water supply.

An abundant plant among the cushions is *Dracophyllum politum*, whose orange-brown foliage develops a dense, prostrate form in the open. But in the shelter of shrubs it grows longer branches and a taller form. Naturally enough, the opposite tendency applies to lowland species penetrating into the mountain regions. Manuka becomes a dwarf in subalpine and alpine conditions. It is reduced to just a few centimetres in height in the least favourable places. But it gets points for persistence: in some areas dwarf manuka accounts for over half the cover.

*

The tenacity of plant life is perhaps no better demonstrated than on the granite outcrops south of Paterson Inlet. In the cracks and pockets of bare rock, peaty soils can develop to support a range of herbs and dwarf shrubs, including manuka and the dwarf Astelia, and members of the grass family. Conspicuous among the grasses is *Microlaena thomsonii*, whose short, broad leaves will form blue-green mats given the chance.

STEWART ISLAND

Small waterfall on slopes of Mt Rakeahua

THE HIGH GROUND

Alpine grassland, Mount Anglem

STEWART ISLAND

The south is where the granite nature of Stewart Island shows out in the form of outcrops, tors and entire peaks of smooth, grey, naked rock. Here, the island's topography becomes weird, almost fairyland. There can be few more arresting vistas in New Zealand than that of the Granite Knobs viewed from the top of the Tin Range — a procession of domes protruding robot-like from low forest.

West of Port Pegasus are the Fraser Peaks, steeper, more conical in shape, but just as bare. Two of them have names from mythology that suit their alien appearance — Gog, the taller at 407 metres, and Magog, 282 metres.

Joseph Banks, viewing these peaks from on board Cook's *Endeavour* in 1770, was moved to describe them as:

> . . . amazingly full of large veins and patches of some mineral that shone as if it had been polished or rather lookd as if they were realy pavd with glass.

What Banks might have seen was the reflection of feldspar crystals in the granite.

In the next century, naturalist Donald Petrie was equally impressed by the luminous qualities of the Fraser Peaks, noting in a paper to the Otago Institute in 1880 that they 'glitter in the sunshine as if covered with a thin coating of snow'. Petrie made his name in botany rather than geology, and he misinterpreted the geology of the Pegasus area when he wrote:

> The country here has every appearance of recent glaciation, and the rounded outlines of the hills recall vividly the roches moutonnees [*sic*] so well marked to the south and west of Lake Wanaka.

It was a reasonable sort of mistake. The roundness of the peaks and rock outcrops does suggest the grinding movement of glacier ice. But in this century another valid explanation has been proposed — that the granite has been bared by physical

Pineapple scrub, Mount Anglem

THE HIGH GROUND

and chemical weathering processes. As the granite weathered, it peeled off in slabs. Geologists call this phenomenon exfoliation, and the process may be less pronounced today than during the ice ages when the freeze-thaw cycles, contributing to the disintegration of the granite, would have been keener. The steeper the slope, the quicker the peeling, and the more exposed the new surface is to wind and rain, which will in turn inhibit the growth of plant cover.

'Hard as granite', therefore, is an expression that is somewhat misplaced in the Stewart Island setting. Clearly the 'rock of ages' and symbol of durability erodes in a wet climate; the clean surfaces are not glacier-induced but the result of intense weathering.

Nonetheless, the island does reveal some evidence of glaciation. It takes the form of two small basins, filled by lakes today, below the summit of Mount Anglem. The larger lake, south-west of the summit, lies in a shallow, rock-bound basin and is the source of a stream in the Freshwater catchment.

In a landmark paper on the geomorphology of Stewart Island, published in 1936, Dr Gordon Williams, of the Otago School of Mines and Metallurgy, declared the lake a product of glaciation:

> It is clear that ice is the only agent of erosion that could have excavated this true rock-basin. The hollow is presumably a corrie [cirque] scoured out by a small valley head glacier, and the rubble that surmounts the rock rim was dropped on retreat.

The second lake, to the east of the summit, is the source of a stream flowing out near the Christmas Village hut. Its basin does not exhibit the signs of glaciation as clearly but it probably represents, to quote Williams, 'an early stage in glacial development'.

Evidence of glaciation in the island's southern ranges is not as convincing despite the presence of a small lake, virtually a tarn, in a pocket below the summit of Mount Allen. Williams concluded that the glacial cycle in the southern region did not

Mountain daisies

STEWART ISLAND

Tarn near summit of Mount Anglem

Granite outcrops, Tin Range

STEWART ISLAND

Bog lily, or Maori onion

THE HIGH GROUND

Ruggedy Mountains from Big Hellfire sandpass

develop beyond the névé stage — a deep expanse of snow yet to consolidate as ice and feed a glacier.

Millions of years before the ice ages it was the sea's turn to put its mark on this landscape — in the time before the mountain-building. The evidence is to be found in wave-cut benches visible to the trained eye at 480 metres above sea level on the northern flank of Table Hill. Another wave-cut bench is etched on to the side of the Tin Range at an altitude of about 180 metres. All of which goes to show that mountains do move, if slowly.

And geological change does influence the way plant life evolves, sometimes by isolating it, sometimes by creating different soils and climatic aspects. The southern highlands — and the Tin Range in particular — possess plants not found at similar altitudes in the north.

Haast's carrot, *Anisotome haastii*, is one such plant, which occurs on the Tin Range south of Mount Allen. Its dark-green leaves taste rather like coarse parsley, and in December, in typical carrot fashion, it produces clusters of white flowers on a purple-lined stalk. Although this species is also found in the South Island mountains, the Tin Range plant is distinguished by its small stature.

Another plant peculiar to the Tin Range — endemic, in fact — is the speargrass *Aciphylla stannensis*, which associates with snow tussock. Its flowers are displayed on spine-clad stems up to a metre tall. The species name refers to its Tin Range origins.

Some plants are new to botanical science. The buttercup *Ranunculus viridis*, which lives on Mount Allen, was named in the 1980s. Its bright-yellow flowers appear in December from within small clumps of shiny green foliage. Another plant isolated on Mount Allen and the Tin Range is the willowherb *Epilobium matthewsii*, which has a creeping habit. Its bright-green leaves are closely arranged along red stems, and its red-tinged capsules produce white flowers in December. The only other plants of this species live in the Fiordland mountains.

The adaptations of plant life not only to cold winds and persistent cloud cover but also to poor soils can take surprising turns. The Drosera group — better known as sundews — have developed a distinctive means of coping with acidic and infertile soils: they have turned carnivorous. The sticky hairs of the sundews, glistening in sunlight, trap small insects, which the plants proceed to digest in order to top up with some of the nutrients the soil cannot readily deliver.

Stewart Island has no fewer than four of the six New Zealand species of Drosera, and they are found in the alpine zone as well as in lowland areas, suggesting that the sundews find conditions on the island rather conducive — and insect life abundant.

*

The native fauna of the alpine zone is not very well known. Until recently, much of the information was provided incidentally by botanists who would report seeing grasshoppers or freshwater crayfish, an occasional lizard and birds of various kinds.

Alpine invertebrate life is especially interesting, and more is known about it as a result of a series of visits by entomologists in the late 1980s. Not surprisingly, isolation has produced a fair number of endemics in groups such as moths, snails and beetles. Ninety-four insect species are now listed. Their diversity is linked to the diversity of the plant life. Different larvae feed on many different plants. This link is highlighted by the world of moths.

Fifty-four moth species have been recorded so far in the alpine areas of Stewart Island, eleven of them (about twenty per cent) being found nowhere else. The others live also in the mountains of Southland and Fiordland. Their larvae are found mining the leaves of an extraordinary number of plants, including leatherwood, flax, Celmisia, inaka, manuka, wire rush, comb sedge, and various mosses, algae and lichens.

The day-flying moths are a feature, notably the orange and sooty-black geometrid moths of the Paranotoreas genus. One of these moths, *Paranotoreas opipara*, can be seen sunbathing on bare rocks or open ground. New species of Notoreas, Harmaloga and Proteodes have been discovered. The range of the bright-orange Proteodes moth extends to the summit of Mount Anglem. Its larvae browse on cushions of *Dracophyllum politum*, leaving little bowl-shaped depressions.

At least two beetle species — flightless chafers — are endemic, and the snail family is also causing entomologists to reach for new names. One snail is so unusual it will require a new generic name.

Larger fauna are also capable of causing surprises. Of the five known lizard species on the island, three are endemic. They include the gaily coloured harlequin gecko, *Hoplodactylus rakiurae*, which came to light in the 1980s during searches for kakapo in the Pegasus area. Reaching a modest twelve centimetres in length, this gecko lives in the southern upland areas amongst cushion plants and dwarf shrubs. It is the most colourfully patterned of the New Zealand geckos. No doubt cats and rats have reduced its numbers and its range. The other two endemic lizards are both skinks, one of which, *Leiolopisma notosaurus*, is found all over the island, including

The exposed tops of Blaikies Hill

THE HIGH GROUND

Swampland north of the Fraser Peaks

the Tin Range and Mounts Anglem and Rakeahua. It is also found on Codfish Island. The second endemic skink, greenish in colour and about fifteen centimetres long, lives on the mountaintops, especially Mount Anglem. It is newly discovered and yet to be named. The remaining two lizards of Stewart Island are also skinks — The common skink of the Mainland, *L. nigriplantare polychroma*, and the larger (up to twenty centimetres) green skink, *L. chloronoton*. As no species have been found in the sub-Antarctic islands, the lizards of Stewart Island are the southernmost in New Zealand; indeed they are among the world's southernmost.

Birdlife is fairly limited above the timberline. Bellbirds and smaller forest birds range into the shrublands, but the New Zealand pipit, which prefers open country, is probably the commonest bird encountered in the ranges. In colouring (dappled brown) and size, it resembles the introduced skylark, but is immediately recognisable by the way it flicks its tail and by the dipping motion it adopts while walking. The pipit nests as high as 1,600 metres in the South Island, so the tops of Stewart Island are well within its range. It feeds on insects and their larvae plus worms, snails and seeds. Islands further south — the sub-Antarctic Auckland group and Antipodes — have subspecies of the pipit, but Stewart Island's population is not considered distinct.

The brown kiwi of Stewart Island, however, is recognised as a subspecies (*Apteryx australis lawryi*), and it ranges well up into the mountain shrublands. In 1988, entomologist Brian Patrick spotted a kiwi foraging in the Table Hill shrublands in the middle of the day at an altitude of about 650 metres.

The same expedition found a kiwi shelter in shrubland close to the Table Hill summit, proving that the versatile kiwi can range to high altitudes. Inside the shelter were the remains of freshwater crayfish and chafer beetle, the latter find being of particular interest to beetle science. The species had not been found beyond the Mount Anglem area previously.

From the number and extent of probe holes made by kiwi beaks in the Table Hill bog areas it was assumed the birds' diet included porina moth caterpillars and beetle grubs. Kiwis do not establish territories then hope to eke out a living from them; they go where there is food.

If the presence of kiwis in such exposed and climatically austere terrain comes as a surprise, what logic is there in the New Zealand dotterel's use of the highlands for breeding? Stewart Island has an isolated population of this small plover, which is not to be confused with its common cousin, the banded dotterel. In parts of the North Island (Northland, Coromandel Peninsula and Bay of Plenty) where the bird is more plentiful, it nests mainly in sandhills and on beaches or estuaries. But in Stewart Island the New Zealand dotterel, population seventy and declining, has dispensed with seaside breeding in favour of nesting on the mountain tops and ridges, where it feeds on alpine invertebrates.

It usually makes its nest in prostrate vegetation such as cushion plants and dwarf shrubs, often in the shelter of a rock, tussock or shrub so the eggs do not get blown away in a gale. A normal clutch is three eggs. They are well camouflaged, pale green or a pale coffee colour, with dark blotches.

In breeding plumage the dotterel acquires a reddish-brown front. If disturbed while incubating, it will engage in diversionary tactics typical of plovers. These include enticing away the intruder by feigning a broken wing or leg. If there are chicks to protect, the adult will sometimes run off in a manner suggestive of a chick — hunched and low-slung.

In the autumn the dotterels return to the coast. They flock in the dunes at Mason Bay when not at their feeding grounds on the tidal flats of Paterson Inlet or Port Pegasus (Cooks Arm).

It appears that in the past, when there were higher numbers of New Zealand dotterel in southern New Zealand, nesting occurred in the South Island ranges east of the main divide, and the flocks spent winter near the sea — a migration the Stewart Island birds continue to practice.

Reduced to endangered status now, probably because of cats, the New Zealand dotterels on Stewart Island are the most unusual birds of the alpine zone. Their story adds intrigue to a little-visited region of the island that vibrates with many strange but true tales.

SIX

Islands of Last Resort

Muttonbirders landing on Big South Cape Island for the 1964 titi season were horrified to find their camp overrun by rats. These were of the species *Rattus rattus*, the dreaded ship rat, notorious for its stowaway habit. Rats played on the pathways around the muttonbirders' camp and ran riot in the rafters. They had eaten everything edible and fouled the rest. It was a plague, good and proper.

Until this time, Big South Cape Island (Taukihepa) had been a paradise for native fauna, which depended on the island's insularity for protection. Bats and lizards were commonly seen, and the birdlife, so tame and tuneful, not to mention plentiful, was reminiscent of old New Zealand. In the following weeks the muttonbirders set about their task of harvesting titi and began to notice changes in the natural order of things.

The inquisitive robins had all but vanished, skinks were scarce, and no one reported seeing bats in the sea caves or anywhere else. Numbers of flightless snipe and the tiny, trusting bush wren were well down, and the talkative South Island saddleback, one of the island's most distinctive birds, lost from the mainland, appeared to be disappearing also. Thankfully, the titi (sooty shearwater) populations were holding their own. The titi's aggressive streak was no doubt partly the reason. As for the toll on the forest species, the muttonbirders put it down to the rats — a population explosion over summer.

Ship (or black) rats had been seen on the island in preceding years but never in troublesome numbers. They were presumed to be the descendants of a rat or rats that had swum ashore from a moored boat. The escape of just one pregnant female could be enough to create a population.

Good at climbing trees, the ship rat is an efficient predator of birds and small fauna. It also competes with the native species for food. On an island like Big South Cape, largest of the titi islands at 930 hectares, the introduction of the ship rat was nothing short of disastrous. For here lived birds rare or extinct on mainland New Zealand, birds that were flightless or flew weakly, having evolved on a land without mammalian predators.

When word of the rat plague reached the Wildlife Service in Wellington, alarm bells rang. Something had to be done, and smartly, to save the endangered saddleback, snipe and bush wren of Big South Cape Island. A rescue mission, led by wildlife officer Don Merton, was mounted in the winter of 1964, with the intention of catching numbers of saddleback, snipe and wren and transferring them to other islands in the Southern Titi group. To capture bush birds alive, even weakly flighted ones, is easier said than done. Mist nets were devised, and tape recordings played for enticement.

Two snipe, a Stewart Island subspecies, were caught, but

both died before the transfer boat arrived. Three of the nine bush wrens captured, a Stewart Island subspecies known as Stead's bush wren, also died before they could be transferred. The omens were bleak. Today, both these birds are considered extinct. Not so the saddleback. Its transfer, a success story, broke new ground internationally in the management of endangered wildlife.

The South Island saddleback, the size of a blackbird but glossier, belongs to the distinctive family of New Zealand wattlebirds. Its fleshy orange wattles sprout from soft skin at the base of the bill, rather like they do on the domestic hen. Across its back, forming a saddle, is a band of bright chestnut feathers. Its relatives are the huia, now extinct, and kokako — poor fliers like the saddleback. All have rounded, relatively short wings. The saddleback's Maori name, tieke, is probably derived from its song, a chattering rhythm. The bird, in North Island and South Island forms, was once widespread on mainland New Zealand, but is now confined to a handful of offshore islands where predators are few or non-existent.

Muttonbirders' camp at Murderers Cove, Big South Cape Island

Insects and fruit make up the saddleback's diet. The bird is a noisy forager, scratching vigorously in the leaf litter and tearing at dead wood with its bill. Rats and cats can easily hear it coming. Fantails often accompany the saddleback, hoping for missed pickings.

In 1964, the South Island saddleback was in big trouble. Its only hope of survival lay in the transfer by boat of thirty-six birds from rat-ridden Big South Cape Island to two smaller islands, Kaimohu Island, three kilometres north, and Big Island off Easy Harbour. Though small (Kaimohu is only eighteen hectares), the islands were free of rats — and the saddlebacks made the most of it. The birds were soon breeding. By 1969, their numbers justified a 'cropping' to establish populations on other safe islands, a spreading of the risks. There are saddlebacks on nine small islands around Stewart Island now, including some that harbour the Polynesian rat, or kiore, *Rattus exulans*. Kiore evidently do not present as much of a danger to saddlebacks as the larger ship rat.

The Big South Cape rescue was more than a coup for New Zealand wildlife managers; it was of interest worldwide as the first example of direct intervention to save a species from imminent extinction. Island transfers had been done before in New Zealand, going back to Richard Henry's transfer of kiwi and kakapo to Resolution Island in Dusky Sound in the 1890s. But none had the urgency of the Big South Cape operation.

South Island saddlebacks are off the critically endangered list now, with a total population approaching 400. In 1992, there was a transfer of sixty birds to rat-free Breaksea Island in Fiordland — a leap forward for the saddlebacks. Their story demonstrates the value of maintaining offshore islands in predator-free condition as lifeboats for the endangered birds unique to New Zealand.

*

Stewart Island's outliers are islands of last resort for several species, among them a world treasure — the flightless parrot of the night, kakapo. Codfish Island, three kilometres off the north-west coast, is home to twenty-nine kakapo. Codfish and a wildlife sanctuary off the Northland coast, Little Barrier Island, hold the last populations of kakapo. A few birds may have eluded the exhaustive searches in southern areas of Stewart Island in recent years, but they will play little part in the future security of the species. Codfish and Little Barrier hold the key, but especially Codfish, which has the larger population.

At 1,359 hectares, Codfish is Stewart Island's largest outlier, cliffed, hilly and forest-clad, and too far offshore for rats to swim to. It supports an incredible array of birdlife — some sixty-five species in all. It is an Ark. The Maori name for Codfish, Whenuahou, meaning Newfoundland, is especially appropriate for the kakapo, looking for a new start after years of terror on the main island.

To achieve Ark status, Codfish had to be cleared of two introduced species — weka and possum. Weka were brought over from Stewart Island by sealers as food, and possums were introduced for their fur. The weka, smaller and redder than their South Island cousins, were removed mainly because they were eating the eggs of the burrowing Cook's petrel, a rare bird in the southern part of New Zealand, and attacking even adult birds. Codfish has the only southern colony of Cook's petrel. The removal of the weka may have spinoffs for the kakapo, a ground nester. Many Codfish weka were released at Halfmoon Bay.

The possums, on the other hand, were all killed. They were judged to be competitors with the kakapo for food and, to some extent, roost sites. The last possum was caught in 1987, three years after Codfish was cleared of weka, and the island was ready to receive kakapo. As far as the kakapo were concerned, this was not a moment too soon. Cats were decimating their numbers on Stewart Island. In July 1987, kakapo were taken by helicopter from the Pegasus area to Codfish — the first of several transfers over the next few years.

The kakapo, *Strigops habroptilus*, a name that acknowledges the bird's owl-eyed appearance and soft plumage, is by weight the world's largest parrot. A male from the Pegasus area, nicknamed Bonus because no one expected to find a bird in the area, weighed three and a half kilograms. In a non-breeding year males average just under two kilograms. The kakapo's wings can do no more than help it glide a few metres from a rock or tree, but its powerful feet, legs and bill enable it to climb trees and steep terrain right up into the subalpine zone. Its moss-green, speckled plumage provides superb camouflage for the bird, which will keep rock-still if threatened.

Both in looks and behaviour the kakapo is a unique, not to say enigmatic, bird. It is the only parrot in the world — and one of the few birds — to breed by way of a lek pattern, whereby no pair bonds are formed and the males attract females by building, each to his own, a network of tracks linked to a cleared space, a focal point for courtship. The males also lay scent trails.

The kakapo court is a shallow depression or bowl in which the male will try to win a female, first by emitting a series of low-frequency booming calls then by showing off body and wings in a complex display. Most of this occurs at night. In prime breeding condition, with chest pumped up, kakapo will boom right through the night. This mating call can carry five kilometres.

The mated female typically lays three eggs in a nest that is her responsibility alone. She incubates alone and raises the chicks alone, leaving them unprotected for periods at night while out feeding. Hence the species' vulnerability to predators.

Just as an irruption of rats on Big South Cape threatened to wipe out the saddleback, so on Stewart Island a sudden increase in the feral cat population in the early 1980s had a devastating effect on the kakapo population. Wildlife staff managed to detect it because they were radio-tagging kakapo at the time. Birds with radio transmitters attached were falling prey to cats at an alarming rate — sixty per cent per year. This precipitated the Codfish rescue plans.

Most kakapo came from the broken country south and east

STEWART ISLAND

Male kakapo performing courtship ritual

of the Tin Range — low forest and shrubland. This was where the birds were rediscovered in 1977. At a rough guess there were 200 kakapo left. By 1982, the population was estimated at 100. Organised searches for them employed — and rather depended upon — dogs specially trained for the work. They were muzzled just in case they got too eager. At the same time, the rangers set out to trap and poison the cats, but no one believed this to be more than a holding action designed to buy time until birds could be whisked off to the safety of Little Barrier and Codfish.

To make matters worse, the population was not evenly balanced. Males outnumbered females about two to one. In Codfish's complement of twenty-nine, there were only nine females. How low could the population fall before it became doomed? Kakapo are slow breeders at the best of times, slower than elephants. Breeding seasons seem to be related to food supply, and may be four years apart. If the podocarp trees, for example, are fruiting extra well, the kakapo may boom. Only one or two chicks, blind and helpless at hatching, are reared at a time.

It will be a long haul to get kakapo numbers above the endangered level. But the signs on Codfish are promising. Track-and-bowl units are being built, and booming has occurred. Food is in reasonable supply, although the Department of Conservation has begun a programme of supplementary feeding in a bid to encourage breeding. Removal of the possums has definitely made a difference. For one thing, the megaherb Stilbocarpa is regenerating.

The kakapo is a vegetarian with broad taste. Some sixty different foods have been identified so far in its diet, including fern shoots, orchid bulbs, rata flowers, tussock leaves, rimu fruit and pollen cones, and olearia leaf stems. The kakapo gizzard is small; all material is finely ground or crushed by the kakapo's stout beak before ingestion. The bird will climb vertical tree trunks for a meal.

Codfish is thought to have room for sixty kakapo, twice its present population, but who can say when this particular lifeboat will be too small for its kakapo passengers?

Codfish hosts another endangered bird — the tiny South Georgian diving petrel, but its circumstances are entirely different from those of the kakapo. This little brown-black petrel is endangered only locally. Most of its breeding colonies are in the sub-Antarctic zone, the islands of South Georgia included. The species' northernmost colony happens to be located in the dunes at Sealers Bay, Codfish Island, where there are about fifty burrows. When marram grass infesting the dunes threatened to crowd out the birds, steps were taken to remove the weed.

*

Of the birds on the brink of extinction in New Zealand, none has created more speculation and intrigue than the South Island kokako, a wattlebird like the saddleback, but larger and plumper, with blue-grey plumage. Known also as the orange-wattled crow, (as distinct from its blue-wattled counterpart in the North Island), the South Island kokako used to be found in good numbers throughout forested regions of the south. Stewart Island was no exception.

Leonard Cockayne added this note about the kokako to his 1909 botanical survey:

> This beautiful bird, now extinct in most parts of the South Island, where formerly it was abundant, is plentiful in the country to the south of Paterson Inlet up to the upper limit of the subalpine scrub. The birds always go in pairs, and are never found solitary. Extremely tame, they approach, hopping, to within a few feet of the intruder.

This last comment could well serve as an epitaph to the South Island kokako. Feral cats and other predators would have found the bird easy meat. By all accounts it spent more time on the ground than the North Island kokako, which, though threatened, survives in reasonable numbers.

In recent decades unconfirmed sightings of kokako have been reported from scattered parts of the South Island —

STEWART ISLAND

Nelson, West Coast, Catlins forest in south-east Otago, and some mountain valleys of the Mount Aspiring National Park region. But reports from Stewart Island in the 1980s held the most promise. They came from the Rakeahua Valley and north-east areas of the Freshwater catchment. First, there were glimpses in silhouette of a bird answering the kokako's description, and occasional penetrating flute-like calls were heard. Grubbings in moss on the forest floor looked the work of kokako. Then came the discovery in the Rakeahua Valley in 1988–89 of three lots of feathers — kokako feathers.

Although the evidence is mounting, there are still no photographs to prove the existence of kokako on the island. A few people involved in searches for the bird are convinced it survives, though no doubt in critically low numbers. Others are not persuaded, arguing that a tui could mimic the kokako's striking call. Tape recordings of North Island birds calling have been played in remote parts of the island, but apparently to no avail.

Kokako are territorial birds, requiring dense, productive forest to satisfy their mainly vegetarian needs. Weak fliers, they leap and hop about in the subcanopy. They nest in low trees, often in a tangle of supplejack or lawyer. Their signature call, achieving astonishing clarity, is arguably the purest sound in all of nature.

But will it ever be heard again in the south? If not extinct, the South Island kokako must be perilously close to it. Should one or two birds be found on Stewart Island, the question will arise as to what to do with them. Codfish Island has been suggested as a potential sanctuary.

*

In no need of rescue measures, thus far, is the brown kiwi of Stewart Island, a bird of indisputable resilience. Flightless and ground-dwelling like its cousins up north, the Stewart Island kiwi, or tokoeka, seems quite capable of defending itself and its family against cats. On Stewart Island the feral cats grow to great size, the largest of them being about twice the size of an average domestic cat. Yet the kiwi appears to be holding its own, thanks to the size and sharpness of its claws, the strength of its legs, and its belligerent, territorial nature. It has an awesome kick, a match for a wild cat. It is also a large bird, the largest of the brown kiwis. Females weigh up to three and a half kilograms, males up to two and a half.

Stewart Island, its kiwi habitat intact, is a showcase for New Zealand's national bird. There is an outstanding reason for this — the Stewart Island kiwis, unlike their northern cousins, are not strictly nocturnal. Trampers on the track to Mason Bay regularly encounter them foraging in broad daylight in the red tussock. Kiwis may be seen during the day, too, in forested parts of the island.

This feeding by day seems to be prompted by several factors. Food supply is probably one. Kiwis live chiefly on invertebrates such as worms, beetles, centipedes, spiders, slugs and cicada nymphs. But because the island's acidic soils are relatively poor in invertebrate life, the theory is that kiwis here need to forage for periods longer than the hours of darkness.

Another contributing factor in the diurnal behaviour is thought to be related to the breeding pattern. Within the kiwi study area at Mason Bay, most birds seen during the day are female. As Stewart Island females, at breeding time, do most of the overnight incubation of the eggs, they are forced to feed in daylight hours. Then there is the question of day–night ratios. At Stewart Island's latitude, the summer night is short, and who could blame a hungry kiwi for being out after dawn or on the beat before dusk?

Feeding by day is not the only quirk of the Stewart Island brown kiwi. Family life is a feature. Whereas the brown and spotted kiwis up north tend to leave their offspring to their own devices within a few months, the Stewart Island brown tolerates juveniles in the burrow for a year or two. At Mason Bay, two adult birds were seen cuddled up in a nest with a two-year-old and a new chick. The chick was sometimes brooded by the two-year-old.

ISLANDS OF LAST RESORT

Stewart Island brown kiwi feeding on beach

This communal living no doubt enhances security. Cats would be less likely to attack a young kiwi if it had an escorting parent. It appears, too, that the defence of territory, the responsibility of the male in northern kiwi species, is shared by family members here. There are some strange goings-on in the Mason Bay kiwi world.

Kiwis as a whole are among the world's oddest birds. They have been described as the most unbirdlike of living birds, with physiological and behavioural characteristics more in keeping with mammals. These include a shaggy coat of feathers as fine as hair, a leathery skin, an ability to scent food, a body temperature more akin to mammals than birds, marrow-filled bones, and a habit of living in burrows just like badgers and other small nocturnal mammals.

Stewart Island browns were the last kiwis — of three brown subspecies and two spotted species — to be recognised scientifically. That was in 1893. Each of the three main islands of New Zealand conveniently had its own subspecies. But with the development of genetic testing through blood samples, the old order is being challenged. The Stewart Island birds, for example, appear to be more closely related to the Fiordland brown kiwis, nominally the South Island subspecies, than was earlier thought.

However academic all this may sound, the issue of genetic make-up does affect the way species at risk are managed. One region can restock another if the latter's population becomes endangered.

Islands of a size that can be kept free of predators are invaluable to conservation. Stewart Island is rather too large for there to be any hope of eradicating cats, possums and the like by ordinary methods of trapping, shooting and poisoning. But the small outliers are a different story. Compared to the South Island, Stewart Island is well endowed with offshore islands. The majority are located in two groups — one off Halfmoon Bay, east of the Foveaux ferry route, the other west of South Cape. Both groups hold small but safe populations of saddlebacks, robins and other at-risk species, which share these

Hooker's sea lion with pup

precious dots in the ocean with perhaps the most abundant breeding bird in New Zealand, a seabird that is resident for only half the year — the sooty shearwater. Hence the name of these islands, the Titi or Muttonbird Islands.

The titi's capacity to withstand regular harvesting is impressive. The birds, in their millions, return without fail every spring from their winter migration into the North Pacific. There are titi colonies on many islands off the North and South Islands, but they are small compared to the colonies located around Stewart Island, which provide the necessary burrowing terrain and cover and, more to the point, access to good fishing grounds. Squid, krill and small shoaling fish sustain the titi hordes.

Their return to the colony *en masse* just as darkness falls is an electrifying spectacle. The birds fill the sky with darting, swooping flight, as if to show off their flying skills, before tumbling somewhat inelegantly into the scrub above their burrows.

Herbert Guthrie-Smith was inspired by the nightly homecoming of the sooty shearwaters:

> There seemed to be a pent energy, a fire of restlessness in the bird, the more marvellous because of an entire absence of any perceptible motive power.

*

When it comes to things rare and special, birds steal the show. But that is not to say other life forms do not benefit when islands are kept as much as possible in a state of nature.

Many of the offshore islands are refuges for certain endangered plants, among them Cook's scurvy grass and the megaherb *Stilbocarpa*, as well as for lizards, which fall prey to cats and rats. They are also refuges for the larger insects, notably a species of giant weta, *Deinacrida carinata*, which is virtually confined now to small islands like Herekopare, off Halfmoon Bay. It is one of the smallest of the giant weta, reaching only about twenty-five millimetres in length. Its future prospects were greatly improved by the removal of cats from Herekopare Island in the early 1970s.

The green skink, *Leiolopisma chloronoton*, flourishes on the predator-free outliers but is disappearing from the main island. Growing to a length of twenty centimetres, it is a good-sized target for predators, with a shiny chrome-green skin. It is also found in southern areas of the South Island.

One of New Zealand's least-known native inhabitants — and a mammal to boot — is the bat. There are two kinds, short-tailed and long-tailed, and Stewart Island has both. These bats are small and forest-dwelling and, because they fly only at dusk or during the night, are rarely seen.

The long-tailed species, *Chalinolobus tuberculatus*, is found in many forested areas of New Zealand, including the tall forest of Stewart Island. Halfmoon Bay is one of its haunts. The much rarer short-tailed bat, *Mystacina tuberculata*, is a stocky little animal, about the size of a mouse. North Island subspecies are restricted to remote forest areas, chiefly on the Volcanic

Fur seal pup

Plateau. In the south, short-tailed bats are known to live at only one location — Codfish Island.

Strictly speaking, the *Mystacina* bat carries the common name of lesser short-tailed because the genus, unique to New Zealand, contains a second species, called the greater short-tailed bat. This bat has disappeared and may now be extinct. It was last reported from Big South Cape Island and adjacent Solomon Island (Rerewhakaupoko) in the 1960s. A plague of ship rats finished it off there. It disappeared before any proper study of its ecology and habits could be undertaken. One theory is that it spent more time on the ground than the lesser short-tailed and was steadily eaten out by kiore. It seemed keen on inhabiting titi burrows.

Bats have been isolated in New Zealand for a very long time — long enough, in a land otherwise devoid of land mammals, to acquire some odd habits. The short-tailed bats are not only the size of mice — with bodies half the length of a ball-point pen, covered in dark-brown fur — but they also behave rather like mice. They scurry about on their short legs, turning over leaf litter in search of insects, digging into humus, running up trees. They also burrow into rotten wood. And like rodents, they are omnivorous, being partial to fruit, nectar, worms, flying insects and even sometimes the young of birds such as bellbirds and parakeets.

On Codfish Island, a stronghold for the species, the short-tailed bats breed in late summer and autumn. Their mating arrangements are extraordinary to say the least. Males, in the breeding season, fly off after dark to occupy separate and fiercely defended roosts, typically chinks in hollow trees. From there they begin to issue their mating call — a repetitive, high-pitched singing. To the human ear it carries some fifty metres, although it may be beyond some people's hearing altogether. It may continue all night if the male has not succeeded in attracting a mate.

Female society, on the other hand, is organised around a nursery colony, which is invariably located in a large tree hollow. Females give birth to one young at a time.

The absence of pair bonds, the random mating and the courtship displays from a fixed position by the males are all characteristic of lek behaviour — a rare thing in bats, and rare enough in the bird world, too.

With kakapo and bats both wedded to lek behaviour, Codfish Island specialises in the phenomenon. What is more, the booming of male kakapo and singing of bats are liable to overlap in late summer — two endangered species filling the forest night with the sound of courtship on their island of last resort.

SEVEN

'Piece of the Primeval'

A frosty morning on the Freshwater Flats

STEWART ISLAND

On the exposed western slopes of the Tin Range, the vegetation is stunted and almost impenetrable

Stewart Island and its outliers fit the concept of natural heritage — a place valued for its wildness, its raw creativity, its capacity to inspire and enthral, belonging to no one yet everyone, and to be handed on intact.

This is not to say the Stewart Island environment is pristine and preserved forever. There are dramas going on, life-and-death struggles. Cats and rats continue to plunder birdlife. Possums and deer attack the palatable plants, compromising the natural way of the forest. But in the absence of major on-going human-generated impacts other than those to do with harvesting marine resources, Stewart Island is a picture of nature prevalent, wholesome and rejoicing in the element of remoteness.

The island's natural values have long been recognised and enshrined in legislation. The Government claimed the bulk of the forest virtually from the outset of colonial rule, and, during his visits in the 1880s, government botanist Thomas Kirk grew convinced of the need to set aside large areas as reserves.

Thus even as the sawmillers laboured to develop their industry, a conservation ethic was exerting itself here. The protection of 'scenery' was in vogue. Scenery reserves were created in Paterson Inlet and Ports William, Adventure and Pegasus in 1903. Four years later came a big push for reservation — more scenery reserves at Paterson Inlet, Port Adventure, Lords River and Port Pegasus (17,500 hectares altogether), and areas totalling 84,440 hectares set aside for the protection of native fauna and flora. Mount Rakeahua became a scenic reserve in 1912; Codfish Island likewise in 1919.

Botanist Leonard Cockayne made his visits in the middle of all this reservation and no doubt cheered its intent. His summary of the situation in 1909 would not be out of place today:

> The face of the earth is changing so rapidly that soon there will be little of primitive Nature left. In the Old World it is practically gone forever. Here, then, is Stewart Island's prime advantage, and one hard to overestimate. *It is an actual piece of the primeval world.*

'PIECE OF THE PRIMEVAL'

Rainforest interior with rimu prominent

STEWART ISLAND

Mouth of Topeheti Creek, Paterson Inlet

'PIECE OF THE PRIMEVAL'

The Belltopper Falls at North Arm, Port Pegasus

STEWART ISLAND

Tree ferns in Smugglers Cove, Port Pegasus

Blechnum colensoi

Despite the impacts since Cockayne's day, the island retains the look and feel of a natural wilderness. To Hugh Wilson, a modern authority on Stewart Island botany, it represents 'a remnant of old New Zealand from wild coastline to scrub-barred tops'. Wilson is concerned about the deer and possums, though, and claims there is 'a strong scientific case to support their elimination or at least their rigorous control'.

Comparisons between the vegetation of the main island and that of the smaller offshore islands offer some insight into what the bush would look like in the absence of introduced mammals. The first ranger, Roy Traill, who had the job for some thirty-three years from 1925, used to pride himself on keeping the Bravo Islands in Paterson Inlet free of deer, despite the fact that the animals could swim to some of them.

Ulva Island, where Roy's uncles, Charles and Walter, were based, is now of great interest to visitors, not only for its part in the settlement of Stewart Island but also for its natural qualities. The extermination of Norway rats, *Rattus norvegicus*, from Ulva in the near future should pave the way for enhancement of the birdlife, which already includes popular species such as kiwi, weka and yellow-eyed penguins. Rat-free, Ulva would be an ideal place for viewing South Island saddlebacks. Their establishment on Ulva would be in keeping with the island's long history of protection. It was reserved in 1899. There is talk of its development as an open sanctuary in the 1990s, a place where people and precious wildlife can intermingle.

Codfish Island, on the weather coast, is off limits to sightseers. Because of its kakapo populations, it represents the frontline of endangered species work. In the future it could be a refuge for saddlebacks and rare kiwis (little spotted or the Okarito brown), but for the moment all eyes are on the kakapo work. Whereas Chatham Island black robins were in the national consciousness through the early 1980s as a result of their brush with extinction, kakapo are in that scary position now.

Don Merton, who supervised the black robin recovery, is a key figure in the campaign to save kakapo. Although he has

STEWART ISLAND

Southerly gales pile sand against cliffs at the north end of Mason Bay beach

more kakapo to work with than black robins at their lowest ebb, he considers the kakapo equally endangered because of its slow and fickle reproductive capacity. He puts kakapo in a category with the panda and Californian condor. The world is watching, and holding its breath.

Extinction is no idle matter. Herbert Guthrie-Smith put it squarely:

> . . . the extinction of species is an everlasting blank — a loss that time itself cannot repair.

More recognition is being given these days to conserving habitat. An endangered species cannot be saved without some effort towards restoring or securing its habitat. To many people, habitat is forest and nothing else. The rest is wasteland. Never mind the unique plants and animals that might live there. And until recently, the emphasis was exclusively on protecting land habitats and land species. The sea and all life therein were somehow self-protecting.

Now reserves are being set up in a few places along the New Zealand coastline to preserve distinctive tidal and underwater habitats and unlock their natural potential. Paterson Inlet — a good part of it at least — is a candidate for marine reserve status. The brachiopod and red algae communities by themselves justify a reserve. As in land reserves, visitors are welcome to explore but not to take or disturb.

The idea of conserving designated areas of the sea coast is new and it requires cultivating. Its merits are not always self-evident to people with commercial or recreational fishing interests. But the fact is, a marine reserve next door to fishing grounds may ultimately benefit the fishing prospects by rejuvenating fish populations.

Stewart Islanders may appear to inhabit a paradise, but like people everywhere, they face the challenge of sustaining natural resources. These challenges include sustaining crayfish stocks and defining the limits for the development of marine farming. Salmon farming has boosted the local economy, but not without cost to some natural values.

'PIECE OF THE PRIMEVAL'

Jointed rush and toetoe

STEWART ISLAND

Freshwater Flats from Thomson Ridge

Beneath the salmon cages in Big Glory Bay, Paterson Inlet's south-east arm, anaerobic layers of sediment — the 'fall-out' of salmon faeces and uneaten food — are over a metre deep in places. Shellfish and other benthic organisms die in these conditions. This was studied by divers in 1989 when an algal bloom in Big Glory Bay began killing the salmon, forcing the companies to move their cages to a cleaner site near the Bravo Islands for a few months. The divers found that as sediment built up on the unmodified bottom of the inlet, it progressively took its toll on the brachiopods, urchins and scallops living in the 'shadow'.

There is a question of scale here. How much development is acceptable? Not only does this question apply to the likes of crayfish quotas and marine farm licences, it is relevant also to things as basic to Stewart Island as walking tracks. How much boardwalk does it take before the sense of wilderness is lost?

Whereas large areas of the North and South Islands of New Zealand have had their basic nature changed almost beyond recognition, the opposite is true of Stewart Island — the bulk of it remains substantially unmodified.

Stewart Island anchors more than Maui's canoe. It anchors in its rocks, rivers and rugged shores, and in its garnishment of plants and animals, the hope of generations unborn that places like this will always exist. Long may its nature stay wild.

Mason Bay beach

SELECT BIBLIOGRAPHY

Books
Beattie, J., Herries, *Our Southernmost Maoris*. Otago Daily Times, Dunedin, 1954.
Griffiths, G. J., *Names and Places in Southern New Zealand*. Otago Heritage Books, Dunedin, 1990.
Guthrie-Smith, Herbert, *Mutton-Birds and Other Birds*. Whitcombe and Tombs, Christchurch, 1914.
Howard, Basil, *Rakiura*. A. H. and A. W. Reed, Wellington, 1940.
McNab, Robert, *Murihiku and the Southern Islands*. William Smith, Invercargill, 1907.
Natusch, Sheila, *Roy Traill of Stewart Island*. Nestegg Books, Wellington, 1991.
——— *Brother Wohlers*. Pegasus, Christchurch, 1969.
——— *The Cruise of the* Acheron. Whitcoulls, Christchurch, 1978.
Ross, John O'C., *William Stewart — Sealing Captain, Trader and Speculator*. Roebuck Society, Canberra, 1987.
Starke, June (Ed), *Journal of a Rambler: The Journal of John Boultbee*. Oxford University Press, Auckland, 1986.
Wilson, Eva, *Titi Heritage*. Craig, Invercargill, 1979.
Wilson, Hugh D., *Stewart Island Plants*. Field Guide Publications, Christchurch, 1982.

SELECT BIBLIOGRAPHY

Papers and Reports

Anglem, J. L. R., *Pearson's Paradise*, MA (Geog.) thesis, University of Otago, Dunedin, 1969.

Chadderton, W. L., *The Ecology of Stewart Island Freshwater Communities*, MSc thesis, University of Canterbury, 1990.

Cockayne, L., *Report on a Botanical Survey of Stewart Island*. Department of Lands, Wellington, 1909.

Cullen, D. J., *The Submarine Geology of Foveaux Strait*. NZ Oceanographic Institute, Wellington, Memoir No. 33, 1967.

Dowding, J. E., *Decline of the New Zealand Dotterel*. Dowding Murphy Consultants, Christchurch, 1992.

Hare, J., *Paterson Inlet Marine Benthic Assemblages*. Department of Conservation, Invercargill, Technical Series No. 5, 1992.

Patrick, B. H., Rance, B. D. and Barratt, B. I. P., *Alpine Insects and Plants of Stewart Island*. Department of Conservation, Dunedin, 1992.

Purey-Cust, J. R. and McClymont, R. B., *Stewart Island Land Management Study*. NZ Forest Service and Department of Lands and Survey, Invercargill, 1978.

Williams, G., 'The Geomorphology of Stewart Island.' *Geographical Journal*, vol. 87, London, 1936.

Wilson, H. D., *The Vegetation of Stewart Island*. A Supplement to the *New Zealand Journal of Botany*, DSIR Science Information Publishing Centre, Wellington, 1987.

Mosses and ferns thrive on shady stream banks

INDEX

The page numbers in italic refer to photographs

Acheron, HMS 25, 44
Acker, Lewis 37
Ackers Point 37, *43*, *49*
Acyphilla (speargrass) 80–81, 89
Allen, Mt 16, 85, 89
Anglem, Mt 13, 32, 80–81, *83*, 85, *86*, 90–91
Anglem, William 81
Antipodes 91
Auckland Islands 15, 45, 75–76, 91

Banks, Joseph 24, 84
Bats 93, 101–102
Beattie, Herries 16, 20
Beech forest 71
Beetles 90
Belltopper Falls *107*
Big Island 94
Big South Cape Island (Taukihepa) 16, 93ff, 102
Bladder kelp 63
Blue cod 30, *38*, 40, 63
Bluff 20
Boultbee, John 36–37, 45
Brachiopods 29, 62, 113
Bravo Islands 109, 113
Breaksea Island 94
Broadleaf (kapuka) 75
Bull kelp *58*, 64
Bush wren, Stead's 93–94
Buttercup, giant white (*Ranunculus lyallii*) 25, 81

Campbell Island 15
Cats, feral 25, 95, 97, 98, 100–101, 104
Chase, Samuel 24
Chew Tobacco Bay 32
Cockayne, Leonard 13, 16, 53, 78–79, 81, 97, 104

Codfish Island 16, 20, 29, 36, 91, 95, 102, 104, 109
Conservation, Department of 29, 32, 97
Cook, James 24–25, 49, 68, 70
Cook, William 36
Cook's Arm 12, *61*, *118*
Cook's scurvy grass (*Lepidium oleraceum*) 49
Crayfish 30, *30*, 63

Deborah 32
Deceit Peaks 80
Deer 25, 104, 109
Dolphin, bottlenose 28, *63*
Dotterel, New Zealand 92
Doughboy Bay *15*, 16, 52
Drosera (sundews) 89

Easy Harbour 16
Endeavour, HMS 24
Ernest Island (Pegasus) 28
Ernest Islands (Mason Bay) 53

Falcon, New Zealand 67
Fantail, South Island 78
Ferns 72, *73*, 75, *76*, *115*
Firestone, Steve *38*
Fishing industry 37
Flax, mountain (*Phormium cookianum*) 49
Flax, New Zealand (*Phormium tenax*) 53
Foveaux Express 32
Foveaux Strait 15, 20, 24, 28, 36
Fraser Peaks *61*, 84
Freshwater Flats 10, 78, *112*
Freshwater River 16

Gog 84, *118*
Golden Bay 32

Governor Bligh 24
Grono, John 24
Gunnera hamiltonii 63
Guthrie-Smith, Herbert, 52, 78, 100, 110
Granite 84–85, 87
Granite Knobs 84

Haast's carrot (*Anisotome haastii*) 89
Halfmoon Bay 15, 20, *31*, 32, 37, *45*, *46*, 47, 53, 76, 78, 101
Harlequin gecko 90
Harrold, James 37
Harrolds Bay *37*
Henry, Richard 94
Herald, HMS 37
Herekopare Island 101
Horseshoe Bay 32–33, *41*
Howard, Basil 25, 36

Inaka (*Dracophyllum longifolium*) 49, 90
Invercargill 30
Island Hill 32

Jointed rush (*Leptocarpus similis*) 56, *111*
Joseph Weller 36

Kahikatea 68, *70*, 70, 77
Kaimohu Island 94
Kaipipi 32, *40*, 40
Kaka 47, 67, 76, 78
Kakapo 28, 85–97, *96*, 102, 109–110
Kakariki (see Parakeet)
Kamahi 72
Karengo (*Porphyra columbina*) 56
Kilbride 32
Kirk, Thomas 81, 104
Kiwi, Stewart Island brown 26, 32, 53, 91, 98, *99*, 100

116

INDEX

Kokako, South Island 28, 97–98
Kokomuka (*Hebe elliptica*) 49
Kotukutuku (*Fuchsia excorticata*) 75
Kowhai 53

Lampshells (see Brachiopods)
Leask, John and Danny *30*
Leatherwood (*Olearia colensoi*) 49, 81, 90
Little Barrier Island 95
Little Mount Anglem 81
Lizards 90–91, 93, 101
Lords River 16, 32, 47, 64, 104
Lyall, David 25

Magog 84, *118*
Manuka *74*, 76, 81
Maori Beach 40
Marwick, Simon and Paula *34*
Mason Bay 16, 32–33, *35*, 52–53, *54*, 78, 92, 98, *110*, *114*
Maui 20
Merton, Don 93, 109
Miro 70
Moa 21
Mollymawk, Buller's *66*
Moths 90
Murray Beach *67*
Muttonbird (Titi) Islands 20, 33
Muttonbirding 41, *44*, 44–45, 93, *94*
Muttonbird scrub (*Brachyglottis rotundifolia*) 49

Native Island *65*
Neighbours, Colin *38*
Neptune's necklace (*Hormosira banksii*) 64, *64*

Ocean Beach 32
Oysters 20–21, 40

Parakeet (kakariki) 76, 78
Paterson Inlet, 13, *14*, 15–16, 18, 20, 29, 33, *42*, 52ff, 104, 110
Patrick, Brian 91
Paua 58, 63
Penguins 28, 47

Pineapple scrub (*Dracophyllum menziesii*) 84
Pingao (*Desmoschoenus spiralis*) 81, *84*
Pigeon, New Zealand 47, 71
Pipit, New Zealand 91
Pounamu 21
Possums 25, 95, 100
Port Adventure, 13, 16, 32, 33, 40, 45, 104
Port Pegasus, 13, 16, 25, 32, 36, *40*, *41*, 79, 104, *107*
Port William, 32–33, 36–37, 40, 104
Punui (*Stilbocarpa lyallii*) 25, 44, 47

Rakeahua Mt 18, *82*, 104
Rakeahua Range 53, 80
Rakeahua River *11*, 12
Rakiura 13, 20
Rata 72, *72*
Rats 25, 93–94, 104, 109
Red tussock 53
Reischek, Andreas 67
Reserves 29, 104, 110
Rifleman 78
Ringaringa 29
Rimu 68, 71, *77*, *105*
Robin, Stewart Ialand 78
Ruapuke Island 20, 21, 24
Ruggedy Beach *60*
Ruggedy Flats 16
Ruggedy Mountains 16, 27, *89*
Ryans Creek 32

Saddleback, South Island 28, 93–94
Saddle Point 20
Salmon farming 30, 110, 113
Sawmilling 40–41
Sealing 24–25, 36
Seals, Hooker's sea lion 29, *100*; Leopard 29, 67; New Zealand fur 24, *101*
Selwyn, Bishop 33
Shags *27*, 28
Small Craft Retreat 29
Smith, O.F. 24
Smugglers Cove *108*
Snares Islands 15, 21

Solander Island 20
Solomon Island 102
Sooty shearwater (titi) 21, 41ff, 49, 93, 100
South Cape 24
Stella 67
Stewart Island size, 13; climate, 15–16; aerial impressions, 16; geology 18–20, 84; Maori lore 20–21; European discovery, 24; seabirds, 28; walking tracks, 32, 113; glacial history, 20, 68, 71, 84–86
Stewart, William 24–25, 36

Table Hill 16, 80, 89, 91
Tasman, Abel 24
Te Rakitamau 20
Teteaweka (*Olearia oporina*) 49, *50*
The Neck 20, 32–33, *33*, 47, 58
Thule Bay 32
Tin mining 37
Tin Range 9ff, 18, 80, *87*, 89, 97, *104*
Titi (see Sooty shearwater)
Toetoe *111*
Toitoi Flat 16
Topeheti Creek *106*
Totara 70, *71*, 77
Traill, Arthur *33*
Traill, Charles 33, 37, 45, 109
Traill Roy 109
Traill, Walter 109
Tui 47, 78
Tussock grasses 80–81

Ulva 33, 58, 78, 109

Weka 47, 67, 95
Weller, George 36
Weta 101
Whaling 25, 40
Wildlife Service 93
Williams, Gordon 85
Wilson, Hugh 28, 109
Wing, Thomas 32

Yellow silver pine 71

117

STEWART ISLAND

Cooks Arm and Magog seen from Gog